ALSO BY
Robert Rodi

. . .

Dogged Pursuit

SEVEN SEASONS IN SIENA

BALLANTINE BOOKS

NEW YORK

Seven Seasons in Siena

...

MY QUIXOTIC QUEST FOR ACCEPTANCE

AMONG ITALY'S PROUDEST PEOPLE

Robert Rodi

Published in the United States by Ballantine Books,
an imprint of The Random House Publishing Group,
a division of Random House, Inc., New York.

BALLANTINE and colophon are registered
trademarks of Random House, Inc.

LIBRARY OF CONGRESS CATALOGING-IN-PUBLICATION DATA
Rodi, Robert
   Seven seasons in Siena : my quixotic quest for acceptance among
Italy's proudest people / Robert Rodi.
p. cm.
ISBN 978-0-345-52105-7
eBook ISBN 978-0-345-52107-1
   1. Siena (Italy)—Social life and customs. 2. Siena (Italy)—
Description and travel. 3. Rodi, Robert—Homes and haunts—Italy—
Siena. 4. Americans—Italy—Siena—Biography. 5. Siena (Italy)—
Biography. 6. Siena (Italy)—Ethnic relations. 7. Acculturation—Italy—
Siena. I. Title.
DG975.S5R64 2011
945'.591093092—dc22   2011010021

Printed in the United States of America on acid-free paper

www.ballantinebooks.com

9 8 7 6 5 4 3 2 1

FIRST EDITION

Book design by Barbara M. Bachman

CONTENTS

SEVEN SEASONS IN SIENA

PART ONE

Summer · 2003

. . .

BRUCAIOLI

CATERPILLARS

. . .

⚒ IT TAKES ALL OF NINETY SECONDS. TEN SLEEK, TAUTLY muscled racehorses tear into the sandy track, hurtling themselves forward at nearly lethal speed. Their jockeys crouch low to minimize resistance; some lash out at each other with their crops, and those hardest hit tumble off their mounts and scramble frantically out of the way of the flurry of surgically sharp hooves. Once around the piazza . . . twice . . . three times, the roar of the crowd escalating to a cosmic howl. Then the horse in the lead sails over the finish line—a cannon sounds, like the pop of a Christmas cracker against the city-wide roar of ecstasy—and my friend Dario Castagno looks over his shoulder at me. I meet his eyes and nod to him, mouthing the words *Vai, vai via!* Go, go on!

He leaps down the length of the bleachers and joins the throng of spectators who are flowing over the railing onto the track, like a wave of human magma; the last I see of him, he's fighting off another man for the honor of pressing his lips to those of the victorious horse.

The bleachers are trembling, quivering beneath the feet of the scores of people who are descending in a kind of rapturous fury. Only Jeffrey and I remain in place, the mass of humanity diverting around us as though we're an outcropping of rock in a river. There's no particular reason for us to stay rooted to our seats; but neither is there any enticement to get up. Where would we go? Everywhere we look, we see only tumult; the Piazza del Campo, the beautiful medieval square at the heart of Siena, is overrun with its citizenry, who are in various stages of agitation, ranging from the merely ecstatic to the kind of violent rapture most Americans ever see only in revival tents.

This, then, is the immediate aftermath of the Palio, Siena's annual bareback horse race around the perimeter of its central piazza. It's an ancient rite, an explosive expression of municipal pride, and both Jeffrey and I find it a head-jarring thrill. Why else would we have ventured to Italy in August? It's the month of the *ferragosto* holiday, when seaside resorts fill up with refugees from every city in the country, leaving virtual ghost towns behind them, their shops shuttered and their restaurants dark, so that American tourists wander the empty streets brandishing their MasterCards in vain. The sole exception is Siena, which has its ancient, inimitable business to attend to.

The race itself lasts only a matter of heartbeats; but there's a historical procession that precedes it—a gorgeous display of medieval costumes, heraldry, and gasp-inducing flag-tossing competitions—that requires a few solid hours to make its way around the Campo. Hence the bleacher seats, or *palchi,* which Dario has obtained for us at an exorbitant cost. The seats are small and hard, yet they're far more comfortable than watching the race from the vantage point chosen by most of the populace—which is within the piazza itself, shoulder to shoulder, elbow to elbow, buttocks to belt buckle.

"What do we do now?" Jeffrey asks me, and I really ought to have an answer. It's our agreed-on division of labor: I'm responsible for all things cultural, Jeffrey for all things sensual. I'm supposed to know which cathedrals have the gaudiest relics, he, which restaurants the highest Michelin ratings.

I admit I'm not sure. I'd been counting on Dario to shepherd us through this part of the experience; he's the native, after all, the one who actually had a stake in the race today—a winning stake, as it turns out. He's a member of the Bruco, or Caterpillar, *contrada,* or city quarter, and he warned us earlier that if they won, he'd be leaving us to our own devices—which is exactly what's happened. It's the Caterpillar horse that has triumphed, the Caterpillar jockey who's now being stripped half naked and carried aloft by the jubilant members of the contrada, the Caterpillar constituents who are now forming a human pyramid to reach and claim the beautiful painted banner, called the *drappellone,* which is the sole prize awarded to the Palio's victor. And it's into this seething well of activity that Dario has flung himself, mind-melding with his Caterpillar brethren as they reach a kind of collective nirvana.

We can't blame him for leaving us. We're excited for him—and we feel a kind of remote kinship to the Caterpillar itself, as Dario has given each of us its kerchief—in Italian, *fazzoletto*—to wear tied around our necks, in the Sienese manner. The Caterpillar's distinctive blue, gold, and green mark us out as being part of the victory today, and we're basking in the association, however tangential.

"I think," I say, summoning up all my powers of concentration, "after the race everyone goes to the Duomo for a thanksgiving service."

Jeffrey looks at me dubiously. "Are you sure?"

"I'm not sure of anything right now. But it's all I've got."

And so we begin our descent from the bleachers into the roiling cauldron of the post-Palio Piazza del Campo. We wend our way out into the streets of Siena—narrow, cobbled, and lined by elegantly simple buildings in earthen colors with terra-cotta roofs—usually the scene of a hundred different tableaux all expressing easygoing Tuscan urbanity. But today there's no diminution of emotional intensity; the streets are as riotous as the piazza.

In fact, the sheer violence of the joy on display takes me aback; I try, and fail, to come up with anything I've seen to compare with it. We live on the north side of the Windy City, home of the Chicago Cubs, so we're familiar with the euphoria that barrels through the streets whenever that team clinches a division title—the kind of euphoria that can, whoops, result in broken windows and overturned cars—but it's not really the same thing at all. For it to be analogous, the Cubs would have to be one of *seventeen* ball clubs in Chicago, each one specific to a certain neighborhood; fans would have to have been baptized in the Cubs church and grown up identifying themselves not as Cubs fans but as Cubs themselves; the Cubs would have to be not merely a beloved team but a family, a community, the foundation of our very identity.

And, oh yeah, there'd have to be only two ball games every summer. And the Cubs would've just won one of them, against all other Chicago teams.

That's a bit like what Dario is going through right at this moment, I imagine. The *brucaioli*—the people of the Bruco— have just pulled off the one thing that really matters in Sienese society: a victory in the Palio. Even now they're parading through the streets, hoisting aloft the hard-won drappellone. People are reaching out to touch it, fondle it, kiss it. There's a new banner commissioned for every Palio, designed by a new artist and always incorporating the Virgin Mary, who is the patron saint of this event. *"Bru-bru-bruco!"* Jeffrey shouts, native style, as it passes, without a trace of irony. I'd join him, but my throat is constricted by an unexpected swelling of emotion. This is, I realize, *seriously cool*.

In the Middle Ages, nearly every city in Italy had some kind of annual civic competition, ranging from the highly skilled (archery) to the refreshingly Neanderthal (hurling large rocks at one another's heads)—but those traditions eventually withered away, worn down by a relentlessly encroaching modernity. Not in Siena. In fact, the Palio has if anything grown in importance and stature over the ensuing centuries. Part of the reason is historical; when Florence, Siena's perpetual antagonist, finally and decisively defeated the city in 1555, it instituted an oppressive rule that all but cut off the Sienese from outside influence. The city was not allowed to grow or flourish. The entire Renaissance just glanced right off it, as though it were under a bell jar. Effectively ghettoized in their own hometown, the Sienese responded as good Italians always do: defiantly. They placed increasing emphasis on their native customs, rituals, and protocols. Chief among these was the Palio. In this sense, it was for many years not merely an expression of civic unity and strength but a tool of civic survival. The Palio reminded—*still* reminds—the Sienese of who they are.

And who exactly are they? In a way, there are seventeen different answers. The old walled city is divided into as many districts, each of which is named after a mascot, usually an animal. Each has its own colors, flag, church, fountain, and theme songs; they're like a clutch of pint-size sovereign states all parked within the municipal polity. The Sienese call them *contrade*, and they are, in no particular order, the Eagle, the Snail, the Owl, the Dragon, the Giraffe, the Porcupine, the She-Wolf, the Seashell, the Goose, the Caterpillar, the Wave, the Panther, the Forest, the Tortoise, the Unicorn, the Tower, and the Ram.

Some contrade are wealthy, some not. Some have ancient, bitter feuds with their neighbors; others have no enemies at all. What they all have in common—apart from an independent governing body and a constitution—is that their adherents view themselves primarily as *contradaioli*, that is, as members of their contrade. Stop anyone on any street in Siena and ask him to identify himself. He won't say, "I am a Sienese" or "I am a Tuscan" or even "I am an Italian." What he'll say, head held high and eyes spitting pride, is "I am of the Dragon."

Today, wearing our *fazzoletti*, we feel that we are of the Caterpillar. And in this spirit of borrowed glory we set out for the Duomo—Siena's magnificent, if bizarrely unfinished, thirteenth-century cathedral.

Unfortunately, I'm not quite sure how to get there. We might follow the crowd, of course, but it keeps breaking up and spinning off in all directions (even straight up; I spot someone actually scaling a wall to climb in a window). Still, I can see the tip of the Duomo from where we're standing, and I figure all I have to do is head toward it.

Siena's medieval thoroughfares lack the gridlike regularity we associate with modern metropolises; they twist and turn, they snake and skirt, they fork and double back. (Siena was the first city in the world to ban all vehicles—even bicycles—from its city center, very likely for this reason; the bottle-necks would otherwise be hideous. Two Vespas abreast could clog the average alley as quickly as a lump of gorgonzola can an artery.) And so it proves that the worst way to get any-where is to head straight for it; we find ourselves, in the man-ner of Looking-glass Land, right back where we started.

I'm forced to fall back on that most unmasculine of last re-sorts: asking directions. In my halting Italian, I interpose my-self between smiling natives and ask plizz excuse but can you say how is to find Duomo, and am graciously bestowed a full complement of fulsome instructions and extravagant ges-tures, almost as though I asked not for guidance but for an ab-breviated performance of Puccini's *Suor Angelica*. But it does the trick.

The Duomo is so packed with people, we don't even have room to sweat. And if the noise on the street was cacopho-nous, in here, under the vaulted roof, it's like having your brains clawed out of your head. You can't see anything either, except the very top of the altar, and the ceaselessly waving contrada flags that threaten at any moment to descend lethally, like a guillotine.

For all the discomfort and incipient peril, the principal sensation is one of joy: reeling, riotous, airborne—yet strangely regulated. I'm being crushed on all sides, but I feel safe; I'm in the arms of something so much larger than I am. Calm descends over me. I'm experiencing a kind of bliss, the quiet transport of being buoyed by a roiling yet eternal sea.

And then I'm buoyed by something else. The service—which, over the deficient sound system, has sounded to me like endless incantations of someone's monosyllabic mantra—

has now apparently concluded, and the vast mass of people has rotated clockwise and is heading back toward the doors. For a few moments, I'm pressed against an ample-breasted woman in the most ungracious way imaginable. *"Perdonimi, signora!"* I holler at her, begging her forgiveness for our accidental intimacy, but she can't hear me, barely even notices me. Instead, she's smiling.

I've completely lost track of Jeffrey, but I feel certain he'll know to look for me outside. Unfortunately, when I'm finally squeezed out the door (I imagine this is what it was like to exit the birth canal), I find the portico thick with churning humanity. I crane my neck skyward, where the first stars are just now blinking awake, and gulp down a few soothing swallows of cool night air.

It's the only respite I get, though, before being literally swept up—yes, I said literally; for a few terrifying moments I am actually *lifted off my feet and carried away*—by a mob of people in the throes of something like a benevolent frenzy. I gird my loins, slip into Terminator mode, and try to power my way out of their midst, but it's useless; I'm like a pebble in a landslide. It's then that I notice their fazzoletti: blue, green, and gold, just like mine. These are the brucaioli; they've simply absorbed me, like attracting like. I give in and go with the flow.

It isn't hard to figure out where this is headed; I'm hoping Jeffrey will deduce it as well. Possibly he's even in the same situation, somewhere behind or even ahead of me. In any case, I can't seem to summon up any consternation; the mood around me is too triumphal, too ebullient. I'm riding a wave of sheer happiness.

As I suspected, we end up back in the Caterpillar district. We were just here last night for the *cena della prova generale,* the big dinner before the day of the race, held in the expansive garden of the Caterpillar headquarters. We were seated at a long table reserved for visitors, while the rest of the garden was brimming with exuberant natives. "This is *our* Palio," Dario had told me confidentially. "We are certainly going to win. We have the best horse, the best jockey. And we have paid off all the right parties so that we expect no interference." He made no secret of the fact that greasing palms was part of the process. Victory in the Palio isn't just won; it's purchased. "Of course," he added, "there's always the unexpected, the freak occurrence that no one can foresee, that throws everything out of alignment. That's part of the excitement of the race. But this year I feel such confidence. The wind is at our back." And that's when he told me he would, despite his kind attentiveness to Jeffrey and me, be off like a shot should the Caterpillar triumph.

Dario didn't sit with us at the big dinner; he'd been recruited to do table service. But occasionally he swung by to see how we were doing and to refill our wineglasses. (Wine cups, actually. It's pretty downscale, this dinner; but then it's an open-air affair, practically a picnic. And there are something like two thousand diners. Which would be a lot of stemware to wash.)

We were the only foreigners at the visitors' table. Everyone else was from elsewhere in Italy—Rome, Venice, Bologna—and seemed to regard the full-bore carousing of their Sienese hosts with the kind of upraised eyebrows a maiden aunt might display at a frat party. We sat next to a couple from the nearby town of Poggibonsi, which is within the province of Siena but since it's outside the city walls is as foreign to the urban Sienese as any hamlet in Asia or Africa, and thus consigned to this corner for aliens. We'd actually passed Poggibonsi a day or so earlier in Dario's van, and the name instantly became a kind of in-joke. Afterward, whenever there was a lull in the day's activities, one of us would exclaim, *"Poggibonsi!"* to the general hilarity of the other. We'd done so a few times during the dinner, too, before we learned of our neighbors' actual habitation there, so I had to invent some awkward lie to explain why we'd been continually blurting out the name of their hometown. "We plan to visit tomorrow," I said, "and we are so excited."

The couple's eyes widened. "You come to Poggibonsi?" They exchanged a furtive glance. "Why?"

"We are told it is so beautiful." I was sure this would pacify them, but they just looked at me all the more strangely. Later I would learn that Poggibonsi is a drab little industrial town. The only tourists they ever see there are the ones who are hopelessly lost.

Eventually the Poggibonsesi and I grew tired of reaching quite so far across the language divide, and we politely drew back from each other. I turned my attention instead to the assembled Caterpillars.

What I saw was a kind of revelation. There'd been a burst of activity when the dinner began, with the medieval-clad drummer boys making a stirringly martial entrance and a rousing rendition of the contrada's anthem, which begins as follows:

Viva viva la bella Contrada
Che di tutte è più grande e più forte
Vada fiero chi schiuse le porte
All'impavida sua Nobiltà.

(Long live the beautiful contrada
Mightiest and strongest of all
Be proud who opened the gates
To its undaunted nobility.)

I enjoyed that; it's what's drawn me to Italians in general—their theatricality, their love of tradition, their *spirit*. Ever since my first trip to Rome, some ten years ago, I've found the robustness of the Italians' appetites (for food, for music, for fashion) to be a welcome antidote to the dismaying anemia of modern American culture, which seems anchored by the Internet on one end and the shopping mall on the other. Being of Italian blood myself (my grandfather was born in Asiago), I imagined that there was something in my DNA that responded to the Roman way of life—and the Venetian, and the Milanese, and the Bolognese, and all the others I've experienced in the years since. But it wasn't till last night, taking in what was actually going on in the ancient society surrounding me, that I found what I didn't even know I'd been looking for: the ideal Italian society. And hence the ideal society, period.

A first glance seemed to argue for a deeply segregated community: there were tables at which only middle-aged men were seated; others where their distaff counterparts held court. Couples with young children were relegated to a certain set of tables, while teenagers had their own dedicated seating, from which they seemed forever to be darting away and then back again.

Yet they weren't in any real sense separate. Because there was one overriding mood in the place: that of exuberant fellowship, of camaraderie, of the sheer joy of being among others who are exactly like you. Throughout the night, small groupings of a half-dozen or more persons would rise from their seats and robustly sing one of the Caterpillar's many anthems—even teenage girls did so, without a trace of irony; teenage girls, perhaps the most jaded and world-weary citizens in any Western democracy. They stood as one, tossed back their impeccably coiffed hair, put their arms around each other's waists, and swayed back and forth while chirping the same patriotic tunes their fathers and grandfathers had been bellowing all night long. The effect was disorienting, as though a group of American mall rats had leapt up and crooned "Down by the Old Mill Stream," barbershop quartet style. There were many different songs, some of them popular tunes rewritten to incorporate the name of the contrada's horse, Berio (most recognizable, the Disney tune "Hi-ho, hi-ho" becoming "Ber-io, Ber-io"), and plenty of choruses of the contrada's marching anthem, which I'd heard many times in the preceding days:

Si sa che non lo volete
Il nostro bel brucone
Per forza e per amore
Lo dovete rispetta'!

(We know you do not want
Our beautiful caterpillar
But by hook or by crook
You must respect it!)

And then the speeches began; long addresses by the contrada's executives. I've been to any number of fund-raising events in my life, and at each of them the perfunctory, monotonous, tinged-in-sanctimony speeches have served as the chief buzz kill. Initially people will sit up straight and pretend to listen attentively. But about fifteen minutes in, they'll become restless and start to whisper, then to murmur, and then pity the poor closer, who has to pitch his or her voice above a steady hum of chatter by people who are now only biding their time until the band starts.

Yet the brucaioli not only listened, they engaged. They laughed and applauded and whistled and called out comments. Again, even the teenagers were on board. I caught some of them standing on their chairs so they could get a better view of the guy at the podium. Just some middle-aged dude in a suit and tie; nothing at all remarkable about him. But they were all hanging on his every word, in a way you almost never encounter in America, where listening is just what you pretend to do while waiting your turn to speak. Some of the teens were even showing real emotion; you could see the tears on their faces reflected in the flickering light. I couldn't imagine what kind of magnificent oratory could so move them. (Later I asked Dario; he told me it was just the usual boilerplate stuff—"Whatever happens tomorrow, we will leave the piazza with our heads held high," and so on.)

I hadn't been able to get all those images and observations out of my head; all day long, back at the villa we'd rented in the Tuscan countryside, they'd played over and over in my memory. I'd had no idea then, of course, that I'd be returning so soon and in the midst of a huge contingent of the very natives I'd been studying from afar, every one of them now suffused with a kind of sacred mania.

When we finally arrive, the Caterpillar district is churning with color—not only the blue, green, and gold of the contrada but the various hues of its allies, who have come to help celebrate the victory. Everywhere people are sucking on pacifiers—actual infant pacifiers, as though the entire community has commenced teething several decades late—because, as Dario explained, a Palio victory is a kind of rebirth. Grown men are openly weeping. I see a pair of fashionable young women clutching each other in an almost desperate embrace, from which they don't disentangle themselves the entire time my eyes are on them. Children ride on their father's shoulders, and teenagers pass through the crowd with liter jugs of red wine, which they cheerfully dispense to anyone who presents an empty cup.

Suddenly the weight of the throng increases, as though we're being wrung through a presser; I'm forced back against the chill stone walls of the buildings lining the street. My first thought is that the crowd has parted to allow a car to pass; then I remember that none is allowed within the old city center. A drumroll rises above the homogeneous din and increases in volume, till I realize that a small parade has formed. As it passes I see some of the contrada youth in historic dress—caps and boots, doublets and hose—marching by waving their flag to and fro, to and fro. These are the esteemed *alfieri*. One of their banners sweeps over my head and glances across my brow, like a furtive kiss. The drummer brings up the rear, and when he's passed by the crowd expands, as if exhaling; I find I can move again.

As I allow the surge of the crowd to carry me along, the sound of the drum is replaced by a lusty incantation of a victory song by an impromptu choir of several dozen voices, most of them either stone drunk or well on the way. Despite the slurring I can just make out the words:

E lo volevi e lo volevi
Sì per forza ma con la nostra forza
S'è fatto ripurga'!
O sudici, e o sudici
Poveri sudici, non lo vincete più!

(And you wanted it, you wanted it
With all your might, but with *our* might
We made you take laxatives!
Oh you filthy ones, and oh you filthy ones,
Poor filthy ones, you'll never win again!)

I'm left wondering about that reference to laxatives: is it an idiomatic expression, or do the losers really punish themselves with the trots? (I'll later learn that in fact they do exactly that, to quite literally purge themselves of the shame. No, *seriously.*) I'm still contemplating it when several of the men in my vicinity take a sharp turn against the tide, as it were. I'm bumped one way, then another, and in the process am completely turned around. Several other people suffer the same incapacity, so that for a few moments we're all stepping on one another's toes as we try to reorient ourselves.

One of them, a young woman with long black hair and large, luminous green eyes, offers a brief apology, then grins widely and adds a little coda. My jaw drops, because what I think I've just heard is *"Siamo andati in culo a tutti"*—basically, "Now we're up everyone's ass!" I say to her, in my best Italian, "I'm sorry, could you repeat that?"

"Ah," she replies in English—clearly my best Italian isn't good enough—"you are an American."

"Yes," I say, fingering the fazzoletto around my neck and adding, "but a friend to the Caterpillar."

"You came from America for this Palio?"

"Just for this, yes."

"You have brought good luck," she says, and she removes something from around her own neck, something I haven't noticed before: a pacifier strung on a ribbon. She presents it to me.

I feel suddenly abashed. "Thank you," I say, and just as I'm about to take it from her, she gives it a twist; the little plastic grip is suddenly animated by blinking lights.

I laugh in appreciation. *"Grazie, grazie,"* I say.

The current of the crowd carries us along together.

"My name's Rob," I say. "Roberto. Robert." Jesus, I'm giving her multiple choice here. The excitement's gone to my head.

"Beatrice," she says, pronouncing it in the Italian manner—Bay-ah-TREE-chay. She offers her hand, and after I shake it she says, "You are here all by yourself?"

"No, I'm with a friend. We got separated at the Duomo, but I think he'll know where to find me. We were here last night, at the dinner."

She looks at me with a slightly higher regard. "So you really are a friend of the Bruco."

"I have another friend—almost a brother—who is one of you. He invited us." I mention Dario's name, on the chance that she might recognize it; she nods in a way that means she's either heard of him or knows him very well or doesn't know him at all—it's hard to say. The Sienese are like that; a bit guarded even at their most open.

We suddenly find ourselves before the stone grotto that marks the very epicenter of the Caterpillar district. She asks, "And what do you think of us?"

"I think you're wonderful," I tell her, meaning it. "The ideal society."

"We think so too," she says, and there's no swagger in her voice, no puffed-up pride; nor any obsequious gratitude for my validation or condescending affirmation of my good taste. For a moment the guard is down, and what lies behind it is beguiling in its plainness. Courtesy and civic pride. That's all. I didn't know they still made people like this.

"And also," I add, "yes, I agree, you are now up everyone's ass."

She flicks my fazzoletto and says, "You too."

A moment later she's engulfed by a trio of friends and is led away by them; and I myself am driven toward Via del Comune, the street on which the Caterpillar headquarters is located. As soon as I round the corner, it's as if night changes to day; the entire street is lit up like a football stadium—only not by industrial floodlights but by innumerable lamps, sconces, torches, and streetlights. People are crammed into every window overlooking the scene, as hundreds of brucaioli and well-wishers stream to and fro, embracing each other and laughing and drinking and dancing, while the chapel bell clangs, clangs, clangs, like a baby with a wooden spoon banging on a pot; it's that kind of joyousness—bold and insistent and not even close to being tired yet.

I start down the street—and when I say "down," I mean literally; the length of Via del Comune runs at as close to a twenty-degree angle as makes no difference—and am fast closing in on the contrada headquarters, which is bound to be ground zero for unfettered Caterpillar glee. I can't wait to see it, can't wait to walk out onto the balcony overlooking the gardens where, just last night, two thousand people sat at tables, serenely feasting, while speeches were spoken and songs were sung and food was served and plates were cleared, and where tonight the scene must be entirely different: a chaos of surging, wine-stoked boisterousness, formless and free-flowing. Last night was the contrada at its most functional; tonight I'll see it with its hair down.

Except that my enthusiasm overruns my caution. I've barely made it to the entrance when a group of young bucks, loud and slap-happy, get into a playful shoving match; I should step back, out of their way, but I'm so close . . . one of them loses his footing and knocks into me, spilling a cup of wine over my shirtfront. He's immediately apologetic, but the damage is done; I'm drenched, and I can feel the wine slowly seeping past my waistband.

I take a few moments to consider whether I might still proceed as planned: insinuate myself into the festivities, drink in all the sights and sounds and sensations. But despite sporting the Bruco fazzoletto, I'm an outsider; I don't know anyone here, and I'd hoped to cloak myself in invisibility—rely on my ability to move among these people unnoticed, the better to see them as they really are. I can scarcely do that now, with a splatter of warm wine clinging to me like blood. Anyone might presume I've just been shot in the stomach.

Reluctantly I head back up Via del Comune, hoping to run into Jeffrey somewhere on the way. Which I do, at the top of the street; he appears with a look both irritated and relieved. "I thought I might find you here," he says.

"I figured you would," I reply, panting from my climb.

"What happened?"

"I got carried away by a crowd of people at the Duomo. Seriously, at one point my feet weren't even touching the ground; I was dangling like a marionette."

"No, I mean, there." He points to my belly.

"Someone spilled wine on me. He was nice about it."

"You ready to go, then?"

I look back down the street—more and more people passing us by, flinging themselves bodily into the festivities like badminton birdies. "I guess so," I say. "I'd love to stay and check this out, but it's trickling down into my crotch now." I screw up my face in disgust and tug at my zipper to create a little pocket of air—as though this will help dry out my nether regions. No such luck.

As we head back toward the city center, Jeffrey notices my pacifier. "Where'd you get that?"

"Gift," I tell him, dangling it before me. "From a Caterpillar gal. To thank me for bringing good luck." I twist the grip, and it lights up.

He laughs. "No way."

"Way. She also told me we were 'up the ass of everybody.' "

"I bet that sounds a hell of a lot better in Italian."

"What doesn't?"

At the end of Via dei Rossi, where the Caterpillar district ends, I take another look back, long and regretful.

And then I let go. Sometimes it's all you can do.

～

WE SPEND THE NEXT few days touring the neighboring towns—Montalcino, San Gimignano, Colle di Val d'Elsa, but not Poggibonsi—and indulging in wine tastings at local vine-yards. Then comes the night before our departure, when we've packed up all our suitcases and set them in the hall for the morning, and we have to decide what to do about dinner. The refrigerator is empty, so I say, "Let's go to Siena. We know we can get a good meal there."

And we do, at one of our favorite restaurants, Da Nello. We've got the place to ourselves, since we're dining ridicu-lously early—we have to, in order to get on the road tomor-row in time to make our flight. The light of early evening is still golden as we depart, so we head to the Campo to take in, one last time, the sheer splendor of the place.

It becomes apparent even before we reach the piazza that something's going on there. We hear the staccato report of drums, the steady hum of chatter spiked with shots of girlish shrieking, and a kind of free-for-all brawling of musical gen-res. When we reach the perimeter, we find what all this is in aid of: a procession—by the indefatigable Caterpillars, the proud brucaioli.

"This must be the victory parade," I say, stunned by our luck at having stumbled upon it. "Look, it's all musically themed." And so it is: there are floats with shaggy-looking rock groups performing atop them, marchers dressed in bulky costumes representing the treble and bass clef symbols as well as individual musical notes, strolling ensembles furiously playing a variety of instruments—even the contrada kitchen workers are here, using actual kettles as kettledrums.

"Why music?" Jeffrey asks.

"Because of the winning horse. Berio—like the com-poser."

"Oh," he says, a bit unenthusiastically. *"Him."* (A few years earlier, we went to a Lyric Opera of Chicago production of *Un Re in Ascolto* but found its narrative too unlinear to follow and its score too dissonant to enjoy; we ended up leaving at the interval. What can I tell you, we're vulgarians; we like showstoppers.)

"Isn't that Dario?" Jeffrey says. "It is! Over there!"

I look to where he's pointing and see, to my astonishment, our good friend—ever suave, ever dignified, ever at his ease in any place or situation—marching frenetically with four other men, all playing flutes and none wearing pants. "Why are they walking like penguins?" I ask. "I don't get it."

The closer they get, the odder it seems. I've known Dario for several years, ever since we hired him to escort us around the Chianti wine country; he was the region's first dedicated tour guide and has become something of a celebrity as a result. He's best known for his old-world charm, poise, and diplomacy, and for the unflappability with which he handles even the most batshit-insane American clients. Seeing him now, strutting about with bare legs and mugging like a clown, is like being thrown into Bizarro world. What possible cultural force could prompt my old friend to so gleefully jettison his trademark dignity?

As he passes, we wave to attract his attention, but he doesn't see us. He's too thoroughly in the zone.

The parade moves at a more leisurely pace than the average briskly martial American affair, and there appears to be no end in sight. Much as I'd like to see it in its entirety, we have to tear ourselves away and get back to the villa for an early night.

Back at the car, I say, "I'm not done here."

Jeffrey pauses with his hand on the ignition key. "Well, make up your mind. Is it an early night, or isn't it?"

"I don't mean tonight. I mean, I'm coming back someday. I'm coming back, and I'm doing all of this over again. I'm not letting these people out of my sight."

And then Jeffrey pulls into traffic and drives away, and we turn our minds back to car rental returns and seat assignments.

PART TWO

*S*ummer · *2008*

. . .

The

FOUR GREENS

ARRIVAL

· · ·

⚌ WHAT WITH CAREER AND FAMILY OBLIGATIONS, IT'S FIVE years before I can manage to return; and when I do, it's to a room at the San Francesco, a bed-and-breakfast set squarely in the heart of the Caterpillar district—in fact, my window looks down on the very grotto, with its sculpture of a rampant caterpillar, that serves as a locus for the neighborhood. I couldn't possibly be better situated unless I took up residency in the grotto itself, which would possibly be disrespectful.

I've also learned that my room at the San Francesco is just yards away from the stable where the Caterpillar's horse will soon be stalled. The animal will have the benefit of constant attention by the contrada's chief groom, called the *barbaresco*.

At this point I could use a barbaresco myself. As I unpack my suitcase, I feel a slight disorientation. Five years haven't dimmed my resolve to know and understand this community; if anything, it's added a new element: to become one of them. In fact, several months ago I became a dues-paying *protettore* of the contrada—literally, a protector—and as such got on its mailing list. I've been regularly receiving notifications of its upcoming events—competitions, parties, excursions, celebrations—which has helped me construct in my head a kind of narrative for its residents' communal lives: vital, active, and above all cheerful. So much joy comes bleeding through those emails; my screen seems to brighten perceptibly whenever I open one. So it was only natural that eventually I'd find myself dreaming of being part of it all, lulling myself to sleep with fantasies of entering the contrada headquarters to shouts of acclaim and throngs of well-wishers. But now that I'm here, I can feel in my bones how ridiculous those visions were; I'm just a bit of flotsam on an enormous current that's barreling through Via dei Rossi and down Via del Comune. I'm no one.

I've arrived during *i giorni del Palio*—the days of the Palio—and the spirits of the contrada are pitched so high, your spectacles might crack if you creep too close. The last time I was here, I had Jeffrey to talk to, so I hadn't noticed the complete immersion of the natives in their annual rite. Now, on my own, I'm confronted with the enormity of their self-containment; this is the time of year when they most fully express their civic identities, when they celebrate their friendships and their rivalries and crown a new winner in their never-ending struggle for dominance. In essence, Siena is a city that defines itself by competition, by victory and defeat, by serious *play*. What happens this week will have repercussions for months to come and will reshape the municipal narrative, reordering the entire hierarchy and drawing brandnew battle lines. Which means that a visiting American, in this place and at this time, has so little chance of making any kind of impression on the locals that I could sprout wings and fly circles around the Palazzo Pubblico without exciting comment.

Yet I mean to make myself known. At the very least I

know there's an encouraging precedent. In the years since I was last here, Dario has published a few memoirs, the first of which contains the story of one Roy Moskovitz, a middle-aged academic from New York who came to Siena in the 1960s, fell in love with the Caterpillar contrada, and through the sheer relentlessness of his ardor became beloved of it in return. Its residents succumbed to his persistence, and to his earnestness and charm, and embraced him as one of their own. In fact, one of the halls in their headquarters is named after him—a room above the museum where the Caterpillar's officials, collectively known as the *sedia,* take their meetings.

If it happened once, it can happen again—can't it? If I can show the brucaioli the genuineness of my fascination for them, who knows?

While I'm contemplating this, Dario arrives. It's been a few years since we've seen each other, so we manfully hug; and there I've got at least *one* Caterpillar to embrace me. (Couple thousand to go.)

Accompanying Dario is an American woman, Rachel, a svelte blond beauty with sparkling blue eyes. It turns out she's from Muncie, Indiana, so we're practically neighbors; in fact, we find we know people in common through literary circles. She's a poet and a teacher and is clearly as thrilled to be here as I am.

I'd been counting on Dario to shepherd me through my initial days as a Caterpillar wannabe, but it rapidly becomes apparent that he'll be spending the majority of his time with Rachel. Dario is very good-looking and has an abundance of courtly, old-world charm; American women find him irresistible. (Italian women aren't exactly immune either.) I learned pretty early in our friendship not to get in the way of that, lest I fall prey to the ire of neglected females; so I resign myself to making my own way as best I can.

There's a dinner at the contrada headquarters, which I now learn is called Società L'Alba. (I ask why; apparently when it was inaugurated, the brucaioli had a meeting to de-cide on a name. They argued fruitlessly until the sun rose—at which time they settled on Alba, meaning "dawn.") Dario es-corts me inside and delivers me into the care of Luigina Bec-cari, who is the wife of the society's president. He actually introduced us via email a few months ago, and Luigina and I have corresponded infrequently ever since, so we're already on friendly electronic terms; she greets me with a big hug (two down!) and kisses on both cheeks. She's an immediately adorable presence—diminutive, with close-cropped dark hair—and is just staggeringly chic, decked out head to toe in typically Italian couture. You know the kind I mean: Versace, Dolce&Gabbana—clothes so singular that wearing them equips you for anything from a papal audience to fighting crime. Luigina's eyeglasses alone are so fashion-forward I feel my knees start to buckle in unworthiness.

Luigina has the Lauren Bacall rasp of a career smoker, which somehow suits her; it adds the gravitas otherwise de-nied her by her small stature. She talks a blue streak as she takes me down to the garden, and my heart goes all pinball wizard at the sight of it again, the trees twinkling with lights, the tables burgeoning with revelers, the banners of blue, green, and gold stirring gently in the breeze. And already there's singing—little clutches of melody from various points across the garden, overlapping one another in a kind of care-free counterpoint. On the opposite end of the property, on an expanse of lawn, several youths of the contrada are practicing the arts of drumming and flag tossing—they must be the al-fieri; it seems strange to see them out of costume, going through their ancient maneuvers in blue jeans and T-shirts.

I've made it clear that I don't want to sit at the table re-served for visitors, and Luigina obliges by seating me at her own table—where, however, she's also lodged two young American students, one of whom is boarding with her. (Siena is home to one of Italy's premier universities for foreigners.) Between Rachel from Muncie and now Joshua and Brian from Los Angeles, I'm spending an unexpected amount of time here talking to my own countrymen; but when I eaves-drop on the conversations of the adjacent natives, I realize I should maybe be grateful for that. My Italian is pretty decent—I've been studying for several years, since my first visit to Italy, when it became apparent I'd be returning here again and again for the rest of my life—but I'm finding the Tuscan accent a very tough one. The consonant sounds are very soft, especially the hard "C"—in Tuscan, "Coca-Cola" can sound like "Hoha-Howa." (This can make for some dizzying misunderstandings; at one point, after I've had a bit to drink, Luigina turns to me and apparently calls me "honey," which flatters me into a sheepish smile; she says it twice more, and I give her arm an affectionate squeeze in re-sponse. And it's only when she gestures toward the platter to my right that I realize she's actually asking me to pass the meat—*"Carne, carne."*)

What I *can* glean from the discussions going on around me is that there's a thrill of excitement over the extractions, which take place tomorrow morning. This is the ceremony in which the various contrade are assigned, by lottery, the horses they'll race in the Palio four days later. The most desirable mount seems to be a certain Già del Menhir; whoever extracts him will be considered to have a significantly better shot at winning.

Another item I pick up on is a bit of Bruco arcana. In the twentieth century, the Caterpillar won in 1907, 1912, 1922, and 1955; then came a long dry spell before the great jockey Cianchino rode Rose Rosa to victory in 1996. If you add up '07, '12, '22, and '55, you get '96. Similarly, the Caterpillar's two victories in this current century have been in 2003 and 2005. This is 2008. No one is willing to come out and say, "Ergo, we will once again win," because that would be court-ing bad luck; it's enough simply to make the observation and allow everyone to conclude what they will.

Midway through the meal, a man comes over to our table and clasps Luigina's shoulders. She beams up at him, and even before she introduces him I've pegged him as her husband. They're a perfect match. He's no taller than she is, for one thing—*and* he's every bit as stylish, despite being completely bald (or maybe because of it; he makes it seem like a deliber-ate style choice). The two of them together are so impeccably dressed that the Los Angeles boys and I look like farmhands by comparison. Sloppy chic may be all the rage in America, but square it up against a couple of middle-aged Italians in tai-lored couture, and oh hell, *yeah* you know where the hot is.

As I shake hands with Giorgio, I recall that he is the soci-ety's president. It's a wonderful opportunity to make an im-pression on a contrada bigwig. But drink and exhaustion have shut down my wit and packed it up in a drawer for the night; all I can manage is to mumble something incoherent like "What an honor to meet me."

The food is almost as intoxicating as the wine: a first

course of lasagne, a second of roasted chicken, and gelato for *dolce*. They eat very well in the contrada. At some point all this feasting combines with the sudden tsunami-size attack of jet lag to knock me flat on my backside. I make my excuses and, while the party's still in full swing, head back up the stairs, through the clubhouse, and onto the street, where lights, faces, and voices come at me all too fast—and then make my way to my B&B. Fortunately, it's just around the corner.

Of course, getting to that corner ain't easy. I've mentioned the steep grade of Via del Comune, and with a vineyard full of wine *and* a transatlantic flight under your belt, it feels even steeper. You'd think they'd provide some kind of assistance for overserved visitors here, like, say, a military airlift.

As I fall into bed, I assess my initial successes: a dinner party, a couple of hugs, and a bit of Bruco gossip. Not bad for one day.

And then I'm asleep.

A PAINFUL EXTRACTION

...

⚔ I DON'T AWAKEN TILL 10:30 A.M. THE NEXT DAY, WHICH is the exact time I'm supposed to rendezvous with Dario at a bar just up the street. I scramble out of bed and into whatever clothes are closest at hand, and zoom out the door.

Bar Macario is a favorite hangout for the Caterpillar, despite being officially in the Giraffe district—an anomaly made considerably odder by the fact that until recently, the Caterpillar and the Giraffe were bitter antagonists. (Even now many brucaioli call the Giraffe "the invisible enemy.") Most of the contrade have rivals, with enmity going back centuries. This can erupt into violence, especially at Palio time, but the mayhem seems almost to have a social function. There's no gang activity within Siena's ancient walls, no juvenile delinquency, nary a trace of hoodlumism or vandalism; why would there be, when all the aggression and acting out that drives such activities are already accorded a fixed place in the culture? In that way, the contrade system comes with its own built-in safety valve.

Bar Macario is swarming with brucaioli. Or should I say, since the bar itself is such a small place, that its entire vicinity

is overrun. Men of the contrada—and it does seem principally to be men—are milling about everywhere, all wired and
itchy with energy; and almost all of them have their fazzoletti
knotted around their necks, as I have remembered to do myself. They've assembled here for the purpose of marching into
the Piazza del Campo as a unified front, to witness the extraction. Because, you see, this is Italy, and theater is in the blood;
you don't just go to the Campo for the event, goddammit,
you make an *entrance*.

Eventually, I find Dario inside the bar sipping a prosecco.
Despite the earliness of the hour and no breakfast, I allow him
to buy me one as well. I barely have time to slug the drink
down before the crowd, as if having received some telepathic
green light, begins all at once to march. Dario and I hurry
from the bar and take our places, and I feel for the first time
the exhilarating—and slightly frightening—rush of being
one of a . . . well, a mob, is the only word for it. A completely
benevolent and peaceful mob, to be sure, but you can feel, as
the kinetic charge of its movement, its sinewy strength,
crackles among the crowd like the firing of neural synapses,
how easy it would be, in another place, among another people, for this raw power to be turned within seconds toward no
good at all.

The most exciting element is the singing: all those tenor
and bass and baritone voices raised in defiant song—led by a
particularly resounding brucaiolo named Federico or, in the
vernacular, Ghigo:

GHIGO: *La corrente elettrica è una corrente forte!*
ALL: *Fooorte!*
GHIGO: *La corrente elettrica è una corrente forte!*

ALL: *Fooorte! Chi tocca un brucaiolo pericolo di morte,*
   cazzotton e legnate nel groppon!

(The electric current is a strong current . . . strong!
The electric current is a strong current . . . strooong!
Who dares touch a brucaiolo risks danger of death, fists
   and whacks on the back!)

This is timed so that the final chorus occurs under the
vaulted arch at the end of Via dei Rossi, where its power can
make your head want to jump off your shoulders and go
shooting into the sky like a bottle rocket. It's one thing to hear
this from the sidelines, something else entirely to have it en-
velop you like Sensurround.

We snake our way through the winding streets. I have only
a rough idea of where I am but am perfectly content to lose
both my way and myself in this fiercely proud assemblage.
Eventually we come up against another contrada, similarly
marching—and if I listen I can hear the songs of still others,
farther off—and then we turn sharply, and here we are: the
Piazza del Campo is spread out before us, like a meadow of
roseate stone. Ringed by ancient buildings whose windows
overlook it as though it were an amphitheater (which in a
sense it is) and anchored by the grand edifice of the Palazzo
Pubblico and the sky-tweaking Torre del Mangia, this is, to
me, one of the most beautiful urban settings in the Western
world. It's suitably imposing, but its scale is human; people
feel comfortable here. The Campo itself is shell-shaped, os-
tensibly because in the Middle Ages the shell was a symbol of
prosperity; but the gently scalloped declension of the pavement also means that from anywhere you stand on it, you can

see what's going on at the perimeter—a technically ingenious means of ascertaining that no one who comes here on race day will miss a moment of the action. Yet the contours of the pavement also serve the function of making it suitable for a bit of sun basking; it's like a stone hammock.

As we wait for the main event, we mill about anxiously on the sandy turf that has been laid out around the perimeter of the piazza to form a track. This is the indelible sign that the days of the Palio have begun: one day the Campo is a carpet of stone. Then, the next morning, you arrive to find this ring of golden earth, set down as if by magic (but really by a team of trucks and laborers working diligently through the night).

There's a long table set on the platform before the palazzo, behind which a row of city officials sit, buttoned up despite the heat in suits and ties and dignity. To their left, the horses are tethered; they're numbered both on their ears and on their flanks; those on the flank are not consecutive and are no longer valid (they mark the numbers used in the pretrials), while those on the ears run from 1 to 10 and are assigned for the purposes of the extraction.

There are two lottery drums, one containing the names of the ten racing contrade, the other the names of the ten horses that have, from a field of many contenders, now been selected as the most suitable. Even among these ten there are favorites, based on such criteria as age, ancestry, and previous performance—for example, a previous Palio victory can enhance a horse's desirability, but not always. Equally critical is the horse's demeanor in a series of trials that takes place on this very course, which begins almost as soon as the piazza's perimeter is layered with earth—the famed *terra in piazza*.

The Palio is different from most other horse races in the

Western world, in that it's run clockwise, rather than the reverse; and a horse can (and occasionally does) win riderless (called *scosso*). The course itself is a real doozy—the most harrowing juncture being the "pass of San Martino," a hairpin turn near the Cappella di Piazza at which it's not unusual to see a rider thrown right off his mount. How a horse accustoms himself to these phenomena during the trials greatly influences whether or not he'll be included in the final ten.

In short, when you take in all the considerations that are weighed and debated, it's amazing that any horses are chosen at all. Yet ten valiant mounts are invariably selected. The Sienese call a desired horse a *bombolone* (its opposite is a *brenna*), and the top name on everyone's list today is indeed Già del Menhir. There's a hush of breathless expectation as each horse's name is read, after which the name of a corresponding contrada is announced from the second drum. (I'm reminded of the line from Oscar Wilde's *The Importance of Being Earnest:* "The suspense is terrible; I hope it will last.")

Each time one of the most desired horses is assigned to a contrada, its members erupt into unfeigned ecstasy (or its rivals into groans of dismay). The contrada's representative—who, in medieval dress, stands before the officials' bench awaiting the decree—is then buffeted by embraces from his fellow contradaioli, as if he's actually done something to bring on this good fortune. The horse is then led from the piazza by the contrada's barbaresco while the *popolo* follow behind, bellowing their anthems at the top of their lungs. It's incredibly stirring, but also a tad perilous. The press of the crowd can be so formidable that there's no room to back away when the horse passes, and the animals are occasionally skittish; at one point during this morning's event, I come very close to being kicked.

In the end, Già del Menhir is awarded to the Torre (Tower) contrada, and I'm prepared for the most explosive outburst of ecstasy yet; but astonishingly, the barbaresco leads the prized mount from the piazza with quiet sobriety, followed by the *popolo del Torre,* all completely silent. Even Dario is perplexed. (Later we'll learn that this was a contradawide gesture of respect for the family of a young man who was killed in an auto accident just hours before.)

The Caterpillar exits the extraction with a horse named Elisir di Logudoro (very much a brenna), and the brucaioli are underwhelmed, if not a little depressed. Elisir is an older horse; you can tell by his name. Each generation is given denominations beginning with a new letter of the alphabet, and E is more than a little senior to the youngest horses in this current crop, whose names begin with I—Ilon, Istriceddu. There's also, I learn, a similar lack of enthusiasm for the Caterpillar's *fantino* (jockey), Giuseppe Zedde. Also known as "Gingillo," which means "toy" or "knickknack," Zedde has raced several previous Palii without ever achieving a victory. "With a better horse," Dario explains, "we might have been been able to lure back Trecciolino"—i.e., Gigi Bruschelli, the famous fantino who won for the Caterpillar in both 2003 and 2005. "But there's no hope of that now." He's too much a gentleman to say that the contrada is now *stuck* with Gingillo, but that's the implication. Instead, he reminds me that the Caterpillar's own captain, Gianni Falciani, believes in the boy, having hired him to race in his very first Palio and even furnishing his fantino nickname. If we can't quite whip up excitement for him, we should at least not openly disrespect the captain's opinion of him.

"And also," Dario adds, brightening, "Elisir is the blood brother of Berio, who won for us in 2003 and 2005. We mustn't overlook that." He's like someone desperately turning to Norman Vincent Peale to thwart male-pattern baldness.

The combination of both a horse and a fantino with long but unspectacular résumés puts a pall over the Caterpillar. Some of the diehards follow the barbaresco back to the contrada, where Elisir will be zealously and jealously looked after until the day of the race. But mainly the crowd disperses like mist. Dario and I depart as well, in need of some spiritual uplift.

Which, in Italy, can only mean lunch.

*L*UIGINA for *LUNCH*

. . .

⚔ DARIO AND I MEET RACHEL AT ENOTECA I TERZI, SO NAMED because it sits at the point where the three districts of Siena intersect. "I thought there were seventeen districts," I say. He corrects me: "There are seventeen contrade. Those are divided among three districts: the Terzo di Camollia, the Terzo di Città, and the Terzo di San Martino." Apparently this is the consequence of Siena's originally having been built on three hills. It's been a long, hot morning, and my brain is starting to throb.

With Rachel is an American couple, Lou and Colleen, former clients of Dario. Over lunch (a light repast of antipasti and *vino locale*) Dario regales them with his patented Palio primer, which I've heard many times but never tire of. Some of the more interesting points he covers are these:

There are two Palii each summer, one on July 2, the other on August 16. Both are held in the same place, with the same rules, and are otherwise so exactly alike that no outsider could detect any visible or textural difference between them, but the Sienese treat them as if they're wildly separate occasions. This is because the July Palio is dedicated to the Madonna of Provenzano and the August one to the Feast of the Assumption. Got that? It's apples and . . . well, slightly different apples.

There is also on occasion a special Palio, called the *Palio straordinario,* in honor of some great anniversary or event. The last was in the Holy Year of 2000. The Sienese are always speculating about what might prove sufficient justification for the next *Palio straordinario.* Ideas are usually shot down pretty quickly; they're very particular about the cause being grand enough.

Of the seventeen contrade, only ten can race at a time; any more, and you'd basically just have a big logjam at the pass of San Martino. The seven contrade that don't race in a given Palio are guaranteed to race a year later—in other words, if you don't race this July, you know you're slotted for next July. ("If you don't get to race in July, why not just race in August?" you might ask. Because *the August Palio is an entirely separate event.*) The remaining three places in the race are chosen, again, by lottery. So if you do race this July, there's still a chance you'll be racing again next July. This same rule applies as well for August. (For a *Palio straordinario,* all ten slots are filled by lottery.)

With this system, then, it's possible for a contrada to race in both the July and August Palii or neither. It's also statistically possible for a contrada to race *every* Palio (as the Ram has done since July 2005; it's the recent record holder for consecutive Palii), though none of them would actually want that, because it's an expensive proposition. See, you don't just show up with your horse on race day and hope for the best. You must first spend several weeks, if not months, engaged in politicking and backroom dealing, what the Sienese call "strategy." These negotiations continue, among the *fantini* themselves, on horseback at the starting line, right up to the very moment the race starts.

The prize banners—the *drappelloni*—always contain an image of the Virgin but otherwise vary wildly in approach, technique, and subject matter. Each summer, one drappellone is created by a Sienese artist, the other by a talent from outside the city. Previous commissions have been given to renowned artists such as Renato Guttuso and Fernando Botero.

Despite my intense interest in all this, it's a little disconcerting that I'm well into my second day here and I'm still managing to speak only to Americans and hear things I've already heard before. So it's a relief when Luigina breezes by, spots us in the window, and comes in to join us, bringing with her a gust of authenticity that seems to raise the temperature in the place by about five degrees. She lights a cigarette and spends a few minutes chatting with Rachel, who surprises me by having a command of Italian superior to my own. (Rachel's mother, I'll later learn, lives in Calabria. "That's no explanation," I'll protest. "That just means you should speak *Calabrese* fluently.")

When there's a break in their conversation, I engage Luigina; I've learned a little bit about her from our email correspondence, but now's my chance to hear it from her own lips. She sits facing me, alert and agreeable, holding her cigarette up near her temple. "So, Luigina," I say in my halting Italian, "if I remember correctly, you're not originally from here, right?"

She takes a quick puff as she shakes her head, then expels the smoke and says, "No, but I was born in Grosseto, in the city of Maremma, so I *am* Tuscan. And my mother had an aunt who had a friend who lived in Siena—a certain Countess Piccolomini—and often she would go and visit her. One year—it was 1955—the countess invited her to come see the July Palio. Which, as you may know, was won by the Caterpillar.

"When my aunt returned home, she brought with her a gift for me—despite that I was at the time just a month old. It was a small doll dressed as a page of the Bruco. This gift accompanied me all my life, including when we moved to Piombino for my father's job. My mother found work in a hospital, and it was there I met Giorgio, who was of course both Sienese and of the Bruco, but at that time I knew nothing of the contrade, and of the Palio I knew only what I had heard my aunt recount. But after I met Giorgio in 1971 I went to Siena and saw my first Palio . . . and a year later we were married and he brought me into the Caterpillar. Strange, no?—That the little doll given to me by my aunt, and which I kept with such affection all those years, was in fact an early inkling of my destiny?"

We're momentarily distracted by ordering more wine, which surprises me, because we've already had a fair amount. In fact, Lou and Colleen now depart, with looks on their faces that clearly read Must Nap. Then Luigina picks up where she left off.

"A year after we were married, our son Simone was born, and that day in the contrada they flew a flag with a blue bow on it, as is the custom. In 1977 our second child, Stefano, arrived. At that time we lived in a house in the territory of the Giraffe, and you may well believe I always brought the children to play in the Bruco, to teach them their birthright!" She purses her lips in a *So there* kind of way and takes a self-congratulatory drag off her cigarette.

The new bottle arrives; by now we're all listening to her reminisce.

"Over the years it's been my honor to meet so many contradaioli both humble and grand, like Signora Armida, who lived above Società L'Alba and who was always at her window, calling out her greetings to all who passed. Over the course of time her vision failed her, but she was too proud to admit it, and though she could no longer see who passed beneath her she still maintained her post in the window and pretended she could. When I would come by, she'd call out, 'Who's there?' and I would say, 'Luigina, the wife of Giorgio; how are you, Armida?' And every time she said the same thing: 'Oh, my dear, I didn't recognize you, you've grown even more beautiful.' "

As our laughter dies away, I'm ready for a nap myself. I walk back to the B&B with Dario and Rachel, but when we reach the doors of San Francesco, Dario recalls that he's volunteered me to work in the Caterpillar kitchens tonight. "If you want to show the contrada you're serious in your regard for them, let them see you working on their behalf." I'm all for that, so before I go in for my nap, he advises that we just head around the corner to the Società so I can be introduced to Silvia, who's in charge of the operations. I reckon I can manage to keep my eyelids from drooping for a little while longer.

We leave Rachel in the bar, and in the Caterpillar kitchens Dario tracks down Silvia, who is busy conducting a cadre of workers so large I'm amazed she doesn't need to use a megaphone, or, better yet, semaphore. "Silvia is the president of the Committee of Joy," Dario explains, and I immediately fall in love with the name; it sounds like the title of a John

Cheever novel. "She's also the daughter of Germano Trapassi, a former *rettore*."

"Rettore?" I ask.

"Rector. The top official in the contrada."

"I thought that was Giorgio. Isn't he president?"

"He's president of the *society*. The rettore is head of the entire contrada."

Before I can ask for further clarification we've reached Silvia. She's a slender, doelike Audrey Hepburn type, but when she shakes my hand and looks me in the eye, I can instantly see there's nothing gamine about her; she has the force of character of Margaret Thatcher.

Silvia says she'll be glad to have me in the kitchen tonight, so that's all set. We return to the bar, where Rachel—whose prowess in Italian is, I'm beginning to learn, second only to her genuine openness of spirit—has already managed to strike up an animated conversation with two brucaioli. Dario shrugs and says, "Well, since we're here, we may as well have a drink," and orders a round of prosecco.

The intricacies of Italian phraseology, and the quirks of its idiomatic expressions, can take a long time to learn. Today is when I finally twig to the fact that in Italian, "We may as well have a drink" means "We may as well drain the place dry." If I had any doubts, they dissipate when, back at the door to San Francesco, Dario looks up the street, sees the overflow of high spirits from Bar Macario, and repeats the phrase, to pretty much the same effect.

We stay long enough for Dario to argue postextraction strategy with another brucaiolo, Cristiano, who insists, "We don't have any hope of winning the race, so we should just focus instead on winning the Masgalano"—the award for most elegant contrada.

I'm about to stagger back to the San Francesco when Dario, noticing the time, says, "You know, if you head to the Campo right now, you may be in time for the first *prova.*"

Well . . . all right, then. I guess I can spare a few minutes. And so off I go to the piazza, while Dario and Rachel head back to their car.

The *prove* are essentially rehearsals for the race and are held twice a day between the extraction and the actual Palio; the purpose is to give the jockeys and the horses time to grow accustomed to each other, to forge a working relationship—and to become comfortable with the ungainly course. They always attract a sizable crowd and manage to provoke a little thrill of excitement even though the results count for nothing. Today's prova is a lovely thing to watch—a kind of energetic frolic around the track—and five minutes after it's over I've already forgotten who "won."

LATER I'LL HEAR A RUMOR of a brawl between rival contrade that occurred shortly after the prova. This kind of thing apparently happens all the time. Dario likes to tell the story of two factions going at it hammer and tongs, when someone called out that he'd lost his wedding ring. Everyone stopped fighting to search; one of the rival members found the missing item and handed it back to its owner, who thanked him, placed it back on his finger, then balled his fist and socked his benefactor in the jaw. And the rumble continued happily apace.

If *YOU CAN'T STAND*
THE HEAT

...

⚔ I LURCH UP FROM MY NAP, NUMB-FACED AND ALARMED. I'm late for kitchen duty, having succumbed, too late, to a prosecco-weighted slumber that needed to run its full course. Not the ideal way to begin my official relationship with the contrada. If, as Dario says, the brucaioli will respond to my undertaking humble labor on their behalf, then I've screwed the pooch already; how humble is it to report for duty half an hour after your stint begins? Nothing, in fact, could better demonstrate arrogance than strolling on in whenever I damn well please.

I pull myself together and surge on out the door. I slip my fazzoletto over my neck as I clatter down the stairs; it's de rigueur for the days of Palio—if I showed up without it, I'd be the only one in the place with a naked neck, which would only compound my original offense.

As I burst out the San Francesco's doors, I spot the horse Elisir, handsome and in high spirits, out for an airing near the stables. Several children of the Caterpillar have gathered to gawk at him. That's the way of it in Siena; the horse, once chosen, becomes the contrada's hero.

I take a few moments to sidle over and join them. Elisir shakes his head at my approach, as if to say, "Buddy, you got business elsewhere," which of course I do, but I pause long enough to say to one of the kids, who's brought a couple of carrots as a kind of divine offering, "Do you think he can win?"

He looks up at me for a moment, as if gauging whether I'm worth speaking to, before deciding that my ungainly Italian is outweighed by my Bruco fazzoletto. "He has to," he replies with complete sincerity. "It's been three whole years since we've had a victory."

I have to stifle a laugh, wondering how his elders would react to such a sentiment. They, after all, had to endure a *four-decade* dry spell between the Caterpillar victories of 1955 and 1996. Within the contrada, theirs is what was known as the *sfiga* generation—"sfiga" being slang for "unlucky" whereas their children and grandchildren, who have now seen three victories over the course of just eleven years, are known as the *culo* generation, after the expression *"Che culo!"*—meaning "What luck!" And this *cittino* with the carrots, who can't be more than seven, is even luckier, having been born into a world in which the Caterpillar winning is something that happens every few years.

My detour to gape at Elisir has made me even later, so I end up loping down Via del Comune's steep decline, to the point that I almost take flight. I can still salvage this opportunity, if I'm abject enough and work sufficiently diligently. I'm certainly more than willing. If every member of the contrada contributes some manner of labor to the common cause—a notion I find hard to imagine, given their sheer number—then I, too, will roll up my sleeves and get my hands dirty.

But no, my hands had better stay scrupulously clean, because I've been assigned to the kitchen—a source of some trepidation for me. I've never worked in a restaurant, never even waited tables, nor am I on an easy footing with the Italian system of measurements, and my home cooking method is basically to keep throwing stuff in until it tastes good. Still, I'm pretty certain I won't be set to work making piecrusts or mixing mayonnaise. If this dinner is to be anything like the others I've seen here, it will be a basic plate-and-serve affair: salad or antipasti, followed by a pasta dish, a meat course, and a prepackaged dolce to round it off.

The sun is low in the sky when I arrive, casting a gorgeous persimmon glow over the trees and hedges that line the property. As I descend the steps I spot Silvia, who's conferring with a couple of burly Bruco males. If I read her gestures correctly, it has something to do with moving the entire garden six inches to the left. I wave to her over the railing and call out, "Ciao, Silvia!" as though she were the person in the world I'm most eager to see—realizing too late that the reverse can scarcely be the case.

In fact, she gives me a sort of fixed smile, then turns to her two companions and says something I don't quite catch—but I can imagine it's along the lines of, Please excuse me while I go and find some place for this American friend of Dario where he can do the least harm.

Even so, she's extremely courteous as she leads me to the kitchens. She's making some amiable chatter and I'm too intimidated to admit I only understand about thirty percent of it. I just smile and repeat, *"Sì, sì, sì,"* like an idiot. For all I know she's asking, "And do you have any experience in the slaughter of livestock?" and I'm telling her Yes, yes, yes.

Please lead me to your doomed sheep and poultry. "And did you bring your own knives?" Yes, yes, yes. I carry them with me always. They are my children.

Fortunately, once we enter the kitchen I can see that the evening's carnivorous offering is already quite oven-friendly. There are chicken parts everywhere, being systematically dressed with olive oil and rosemary. I'm introduced to the chef, who's called Biondo, which means "Blond"—despite which his hair is carrot red. (Later I'll learn the nickname comes from a restaurant he used to own, Il Biondo in Via Montanini.) He's a tall, broad-shouldered man in his forties who smiles and welcomes me with carefully pronounced consonants, perhaps having been forewarned of my stupidity. Then I meet another worker, Antonella, in whose lap Silvia more or less deposits me before beating a hasty (yet elegant) retreat. Antonella is a pleasant-faced woman with golden ringlets who asks me to wait a moment while she finishes ladling a large tray of lasagne with meat sauce, during which time there is a small silence that proves awkward only for me, as I'm the only one standing around doing nothing. I decide to fill it by asking Antonella if she is in fact a native-born Caterpillar, which must be akin to visiting a convent and asking one of the nuns if she is in fact a virgin.

"*Sì, sì,*" she tells me with a proud toss of her head, "*sono bruca pura.*" I am a pure Caterpillar. I feel suddenly stung, as though she's stressed her inviolate bloodline over the kind of compromised-at-best status I myself might achieve, if I'm lucky; but then I realize it's just civic pride again, no different from a Manhattanite boasting about being a native New Yorker. (Even Luigina herself isn't bruca pura.)

It's very warm in the kitchens, and I feel my skin prickle

and flush, then bead up. I hope I won't be asked to wear an apron, because lashing me into yet another layer of fabric is only going to aggravate the problem. When I think no one's looking, I swipe my arm over my forehead, and it comes away glistening and slick. I slip my fazzoletto off my neck and stuff it into my back pocket; I don't want to soil it with my sweat.

Having finished the tray of lasagne, Antonella takes me to the very back of the kitchen—where the air is thickest—to a counter on which two dozen loaves of bread are piled high. There's a cutting board with a serrated knife resting on it, and a basket containing a small quantity of bread slices. Half a loaf sits primly next to the knife. Clearly, someone has abandoned this post—probably to attend to something more urgent.

Antonella asks me if I'm able to cut the bread—as though my awkwardness with the Tuscan dialect might be symptomatic of an overall ineptitude that extends to my motor skills. I assure her I can cut these loaves of bread very well indeed, that I have been complimented on my carving skills, and am just short of claiming to have won awards for it when I regain control of myself and shut up. Satisfied, she smiles and leaves me to it.

I start in on the unfinished loaf, carefully examining the pieces that have already been sliced so that I can match their width with mathematical precision. Antonella will surely be astonished by the uniformity of my work. Possibly I will be asked to give a short seminar on bread cutting afterward. I start to rehearse it in my head, so that when the time comes I'll have the proper vocabulary at hand. While I'm trying to think of the Italian for "calibrate," I carelessly produce an uneven slice. I can't put it into the basket with the others; it isn't worthy. Not knowing what else to do with it, I stuff it into my mouth. Mm. Pretty good. Nice crust.

I work my way through the loaves, eating my mistakes, until I've filled several baskets for distribution to the tables. My slices are models of conformity; each one contains almost exactly the same amount of bread. I've even allowed for the curve of the loaf by cutting slightly thicker pieces toward the ends. It is a masterwork of egalitarianism; no one who partakes of my bread will be at a disadvantage to his neighbor. All will receive an equal share. I'm puffed up with pride and wonder why I didn't try my hand at kitchen work years ago. I could have had my own reality show by now. As I clear the crumbs from the work surface, I debate the merits of signing with Bravo over the Food Network.

I've worked up a sheen of good, honest sweat, so I run my arm over my forehead again to make myself presentable, then catch Antonella's eye and motion her over. I display my brimming baskets and smile. She smiles as well—though not with quite the sense of awe I'd hoped—and gives me an odd kind of look, like she doesn't know what to make of me.

"You're bored now?" she says. "You want to try something else?"

I blink. Does she not see my artistically arranged baskets? I gesture toward them and say, "Well, yes. Because I'm done here."

Her eyes flicker tellingly past me, then meet mine again with an even more questioning look.

I turn and notice for the first time resting against the wall an enormous sack of bread. There must be three hundred loaves in there. I don't know how I can possibly have missed it before. It's the size of a body bag.

"Oh, sweet Jesus," I blurt out. "I didn't even see those. Of course I'll finish the job." Embarrassed, I fumble one of the topmost loaves out of the sack and start hacking away at it.

"It's all right if you'd prefer not," she says.

Oh, no, I think; nosiree, no bruca pura is going to get the chance to tell her friends about the shiftless Americano who couldn't even finish a simple task like cutting a hundred thousand pieces of bread. Nuh-uh. I came here to win these people over, and that's what I'm going to do. They asked me to slice, goddammit. I. WILL. SLICE.

"Thank you," I reassure her, "I'm fine." And she leaves me sawing madly away at the crust, sending golden flakes flying everywhere, like sparks.

Now my embarrassment has twined with the closeness of the air to make me sweat in earnest. Pools collect in my eyebrows and in the tip of my beard and start to drip onto the floor at my feet. I have to stand several inches away from the cutting board so that they don't splatter right onto the bread. That means I have to extend my arm all the way to hold the loaf, which makes it look as though I'm afraid something's going to jump out of it and bite me.

The ungainliness of this approach makes it nearly impossible to cut the slices with any degree of regularity, so that soon I'm producing carbuncle-shaped hunks that look like a species of albino sponge. But what can I do? I can't stand any closer without contaminating the bread with my schvitzing, and even if I could, I don't have time for exactitude—I've got too many loaves to get through. Every time I check the bag, there seem to be even more of them brimming over the top, as if it's the sack Jesus blessed when he fed the multitude.

I cast furtive glances over my shoulder. Everyone else is

working away quite contentedly, laughing and joking, and no one appears to be gushing great quantities of their bodily fluids. What in God's name is wrong with me? Why am I the only freak who's sweating like a packhorse? Fortunately, I'm wearing all black, so the widening stains at my collar and under my arms aren't likely to show. If I can just quietly keep working, maybe I'll stay beneath everyone's radar; no one will even notice me . . .

"Hello," says someone, interrupting me in midthought. I whirl with a start and almost slip on the small reservoir beneath my feet.

A young man is standing at my shoulder; midtwenties, a head full of dark, curly hair, a pleasant smile. I return his hello, realizing only now that he's addressed me in English.

"My name is Duccio," he says, also in English.

"Lucio?" I ask, thinking I've misheard him.

"Duccio," he corrects me. "It is a Tuscan name." In other words: you're an outsider. I lift my hands—covered with sweat and crumbs—to show him I'm in no fit condition to shake. He nods and says, "Silvia told me you had arrived. I am in charge of the kitchen tonight; I'm sorry I wasn't here to greet you." He plonks an open bottle of red wine and a plastic cup next to the cutting board. "Thank you for your help. Please let me know if there is anything you need."

"I will," I say, and he gives me one last smile before he turns to go. As soon as he does, I'm free to flick away the drop of sweat I feel hanging from the tip of my nose. With any luck, he never even noticed it.

The wine is a very civilized gesture and reduces my anxiety somewhat; it's also exactly what I need right now, because all the bread I've eaten has rather lodged in my gullet. It feels good to wash it down, especially with something so rich and smooth and . . . and . . . .

. . . and warm. I realize after only two or three swallows that it's having an entirely disastrous effect on my body temperature. I was sweating profusely before; now it's as though I'm made of wax. Sweat runs into my ears and down my neck. It collects in the little V beneath my lower back. It moistens my socks inside my shoes. When I shift my footing, I squish. And beneath my feet is a virtual pond; it must look as if I've wet my pants over and over.

And I still have dozens of loaves to go.

I'm not going to make it; I can feel it. I can't be in this much physical distress without something bad happening. I'll swoon, or faint, or—I don't know, just collapse inward, dissolve into a little gelatinous blob.

I put down the knife and try to pull myself together. Panicking isn't going to help. I force myself to relax my shoulder muscles and take a few deep breaths. I remind myself that the sweat glands are the body's own air-conditioning system. Sweat is what cools us down when we're overheated. Sweat is our *friend*. Soon I will have regained my equilibrium, and I will feel perfectly fine . . . .

Twenty minutes pass, and screw that science shit, IT'S NOT WORKING. I can't move at all without creating a fine spray in the air behind me. Anyone taking even the slightest glance my way must notice how alarmingly drenched in perspiration I am. My only comfort is that the kitchen is now in full swing—the dinner service is under way—so no one's likely to look at me, not even when they come rushing over for my baskets of bread. I'm at least safe from that mortification.

"*Rob!*" calls a voice from across the kitchen, shattering even this small comfort.

I turn, and there at the doorway stand Dario and Rachel. They look crisp, cool, and collected, as though they've just stepped out of the shower and into freshly dry-cleaned clothes. Rachel even carries a jacket over one arm. I glare at them in horror.

I manage to smile and give them a wave, creating a shimmering mist along the arc of my arm.

"How's it going?" Dario calls out.

"Great!" I say, willing him not to come any closer.

"We're just on our way to dinner," he says.

I wrinkle my brow in confusion. "You're not eating here?"

"No," he says, grinning. "Someplace quieter."

I blink. Twice. And I feel a twinge of unaccountable irritation. He got me this job from Hell, and now he's bolting? All because he'd rather conduct his romance in a place where there aren't eighteen hundred people who all know him by name?

But this flash of annoyance passes as quickly as it came. I remind myself that this isn't about me; or rather it is, but it's about the extent to which I can submit, submerge, sublimate—give myself over to a higher cause, become a small part of something grander and greater.

Accordingly I give Rachel a wink and tell her to have a good time, and she beams me a dazzling smile in return. And then she and Dario—apparitions of the outside world, a place of caressing breezes and billowing hair to which I hope someday to return—go on their way and leave me to discover how much more bread I can slice before I sputter down the floor drain entirely.

But salvation is soon at hand; Duccio comes to me and, again in his impeccable English, says, "I think that is enough bread for tonight. Would you like to join us for dinner?"

"Thank you, yes," I say, and I realize that I am in fact quite hungry. My extreme discomfort has distracted me from it, but the fragrant aromas of the lasagne and the chicken have been tantalizing me. I'd salivate if I had any bodily fluids left.

I give my face a quick rinse in the bathroom sink—what the hell, my entire head; it needs it—then towel dry and join the rest of the staff, who have already sat down at one of the prep tables and begun tucking in. Typically for Tuscans, they've done so in style, with a bottle of wine every few inches and a little vase of sunflowers in the middle.

Here's my reward, I tell myself; I've labored like a goat all night, now I'll be welcomed into the fold and invited to tell my story in my halting Italian. My passionate interest in these people will finally be repaid by their curiosity about me.

But no. They're not so easily diverted. They're tremendously polite, of course, and make certain I have plenty to eat and drink, and if I ask a question they answer it as fully as I could wish; but otherwise they go their own garrulous way, chattering back and forth at a velocity I can't even begin to follow, a babbling brook of conversation in which nary a consonant is allowed to impede the flow. Occasionally the entire table bursts into riotous laughter, and I really wish I knew why. I could ask, of course, but is there anything in the world glummer than the guy who needs to have the jokes explained?

Eventually I finish my meal and quietly rise and slip away. The others are now well into their wine and so don't notice me in time to protest; or perhaps they simply respect me enough to allow me the freedom to go.

I suppose my job here is completed, but despite the toll it's taken on me, I don't really feel I've done enough. I haven't bent sufficiently low, made adequate obeisance, to attract even a modicum of approbation from the brucaioli. I have to keep at it until someone, anyone, turns to me and . . . what? Offers a hand? Smiles in appreciation? Remembers my name?

I sigh and begin clearing tables. It's not really necessary; there's a whole complement of teenagers assigned to the task, and they're doing it with gusto (something I again find remarkable, as American teenagers would have to be threatened, possibly at gunpoint, into taking on this chore—and would then retaliate by performing it with a sullen attitude and half-assed results). All the same, I plunge in, choosing the far end of the garden to begin my operations, as the keen teens don't seem to be ranging this far afield.

It's a cool, quiet night, with the twinkling stars melding into the glimmering lights over the lawn; I can feel my skin start to dry, and it's a pleasant sensation. I pull my fazzoletto from my pocket and slip it back over my head, so I don't look out of place. It's a whole field of blue, green, and gold, tumbling down backs, draping over shoulders, tucked jauntily under chins. Leave it to a group of Italians to come up with a means of expressing civic pride through an accessory. Some of the fazzoletti are visibly threadbare, faded, and frayed; but this is highly respected, as it bespeaks a long and active life in the contrada.

Most of the diners have finished feasting—just a few stragglers are still idly nibbling from their gelato cups—and many are leaning back in their chairs, smoking or enjoying the dregs of the wine and passing the time in conversation. As before, the tables are self-segregated; middle-aged men have congregated with other middle-aged men, matrons with matrons, adolescents with adolescents, and couples with very young children among others similarly blessed. Luigina seems to be the reigning queen of a whole group of smartly clad women who are arrayed around her, their well-shod legs crossed at the knee, coolly conversing while holding their cigarettes about an inch above their temples. Occasionally I spot a husband and wife together, but in such cases it seems inevitable that the woman has confidently invaded the male world by plonking herself among her spouse's colleagues; I don't see any man who has dared to seat himself at one of the ladies' tables.

As I collect the soiled plates, I feel an almost clandestine thrill; I'm moving among the crowd invisibly, observing the natives, mentally cataloguing them and committing snatches of their conversations to memory. They don't for a moment feel the searing intensity of my attention.

I wend my way close to the table where the Caterpillar officials are seated. Every contrada is like a mini–sovereign state, with its own governing body, constitution, and elected officers, the top honcho being the rettore, or rector (though the Caterpillar is the only one to so designate its chief executive; the Goose has a *governatore* and all the others a *priore*).

According to Dario, the current rector is the youngest the Caterpillar has ever had; so it doesn't take long to pick him out. He looks to be in no more than his very early forties; he has a head of loose auburn hair and a patient, attentive demeanor. Fabio Pacciani is his name. The man next to him— older, graying, with a bushy mustache and steely, formidable gaze—must be Giovanni Falciani, better known as Gianni, the *capitano* or captain. As I understand it, the rector's responsibility is the daily running of the contrada, while the captain's is winning the Palio. No wonder the set of Gianni's jaw is so tight at the moment. This morning's extraction must have been less than optimal for him. Still, as I understand it, a good captain always has a backup plan. You can almost see the wheels spinning behind his glasses.

Suddenly Fabio looks up and his eyes meet mine. I'm frozen. I've been absolutely busted, staring dumbly at the big shots. After what seems an interminable moment, he smiles and nods. I smile back, then hurriedly resume my rounds.

If I'd had my wits about me, I'd have gone up and introduced myself. But I was too deeply immersed in the role I'd assumed for the day; I was a kitchen worker with an arm full of table trash—who was I to dare foist myself on capital-A Authority?

It takes me a few minutes to recall the bracing egalitarianism of the contrada; here there are no divisions based on education or occupation—the only credential that counts is that of contrada affiliation. Which I don't have by birth but am making a bid for by choice; and I'm here to prove I mean it.

And so, after engaging some of the other diners I encounter on my rounds—including an elderly couple who can barely breathe from laughing once they hear I'm from Chicago ("Chee-cah-go? . . . Really? It's really called that?"— I later learn that *Ci cago* is Italian for "I shit there"), I'm sufficiently emboldened to seize the moment when I see Fabio coming through the crowd, smiling benevolently and greeting all those who call out to him.

"Ciao, Fabio," I say when he's within range. I extend my hand and add, "My name's Robert, I'm an American visitor." He shakes my hand, all the while eyeing the big bag of trash I'm toting with me.

"We don't ask all our visitors to help clean up, I hope," he says.

"I volunteered," I assure him, and then . . . I can't think of anything else to say. After an awkward pause he gracefully takes the reins, thanking me for pitching in and hoping I have an enjoyable stay.

And then he's called away by another of his admiring constituency.

I bask for a moment in this important first impression I've made. I make a mental note for future reference: when striving to convey humility, clutching a sack of garbage is goddamn *golden*.

$\mathcal{T}$RIALS and $\mathcal{T}$RIBULATIONS

. . .

OVER THE NEXT TWO DAYS I MAKE A POINT OF ATTENDING every prova and pay close attention so that I might glean some bit of information I can then pass along to interested brucaioli—cheerfully ignoring the fact that I know nothing about horseflesh, the fantini, or, well, anything at all, really. It also ignores the fact that there are plenty of brucaioli on hand at these trials, so I'm scarcely needed as a source of intel.

As fate would have it, I miss my only real chance at realizing this plan, at a midday prova on my third day in town. I'm already in the Campo, having staked out a shady place from which to watch, when Dario calls me; he's forgotten to get the tickets for tomorrow's big dinner—the *cena della prova generale,* the dinner for the general trial, on the eve of the Palio. He's at home in Vagliagli and is unlikely to make it to Siena today; would I mind very much purchasing the tickets for him? I agree, of course, but I'm low on cash; I'll need to go to an ATM. There are still fifteen minutes or so till the trial starts, so I may as well do that now. I leave the Campo, withdraw the cash, and head back—only to find the piazza closed off. I didn't know they did that, and I'm not sure why they do. Even worse, the entrance is packed about eight deep with those who have been denied access, so I can't even get close enough to plead my case.

Now there's a slight roar of approval from the crowd within, so I know the fantini must be riding out; and, eager to see them, I skitter up the street to an alley that leads under the bleachers and from there try to peer between the ankles of those seated over me. It's pretty much useless; I can get only fleeting glimpses of the track.

The race starts, and I can hear the thundering of the hooves as they pound by me—then a startled outcry from the crowd. "What?" I say aloud. "What happened? What what what?" My head darts like a salamander's between pants legs and panty hose, but I can't make anything out. It's a pretty decent metaphor for my current existential condition: on the outside, peering in, certain of something remarkable just beyond but unable to see much of it.

Later I'll discover that the startled outcry was due to the Ram's horse slipping. The soft turf, still holding the moisture of a recent rainfall, is blamed. I'll learn all this from reading the front-page headlines of the Sienese dailies on display at the news vendors. From this point on, Palio news will consume pretty much all their coverage. If there's a war or a plague or a flood or a terrorist attack elsewhere in the world . . . well, I'll hear about it on August 17.

At that night's contrada dinner I'm once again paired up with Joshua, but by now I'm actually happy to see him. He and I compare notes on how difficult it is to break through the wall of Sienese reserve. They're a lovely people, and we both adore them, but they're invincibly self-contained. It's one of the things that make them so attractive to me; that's the paradox right there.

The following day I awaken to a steady rain. In spite of this I set out for the Campo to watch the prova; but it's canceled due to weather, leaving me with nothing to do.

When the skies clear in early afternoon, Dario calls and arranges to meet in Società L'Alba. I find him at the bar, of course, and he treats me to a prosecco. I give him the tickets for the dinner, and we both look dubiously at the sky, which glowers threateningly, and wonder whether it will actually take place. The tables are all set up and are covered with plastic sheeting to keep them dry till the appointed time; but that's presuming the appointed time will be any drier.

"It wouldn't surprise me if the dinner was called off," he says, a bit dispiritingly. "This is what we call a Quattro Verdi Palio—because four of the participating contrade have green among their colors. Every time there's a Quattro Verdi, it brings a chain of bad luck." Suddenly I recall the Ram horse slipping in yesterday's prova, which I mention to Dario. Of course he's already heard of it, and he nods in confirmation. "Yes, and before that, there was the sad death of the young man of the Tower. But wait. There will be other misfortunes, both trivial and tragic."

As if on cue, I've no sooner returned to my room at the San Francesco than the sky opens like a piñata and an epic storm commences. I pass the hours boning up on Sienese history, but the rain outside my window doesn't lessen in intensity. Eventually it becomes apparent that the *cena* will have to be called off. I'm crestfallen; the dinner five years ago was one of the most joyous nights of my life. But the Caterpillar aren't suffering alone; every other contrada in the city hosts an enormous outdoor dinner for all its members and guests and will thus be equally inconvenienced. But at least they can all hunker down in the comfort of their own homes; I'm stuck at the B&B and have nothing in the way of alternative plans. I'll probably end up darting through the rain for a *panino,* which I'll eat in my room while seated cross-legged on the bed, watching a movie on my laptop.

I'm rescued from this sad fate by Dario, who calls and tells me to pack a bag; I'll dine with him and Rachel in his village, then spend the night at his house.

Dario lives in a small town in Chianti called Vagliagli, a name that seems to defeat any English speaker who attempts to pronounce it. (It's perfectly simple, really: val-YAL-yee. It means "valley of garlic.") Despite this, it's pretty much every American's fantasy of a town in Chianti; it's nestled in a little clutch of hills, like the crook of two plump arms, and its quiet streets are amicably patrolled by old women in shawls whose eagle eyes miss nothing that occurs on their watch. They probably know of my arrival in town before I've even gotten out of Dario's van.

We go for a drink at the village pub, Bar San Cristoforo, run by a pleasant woman named Maria who seems actually to remember me from five years ago. Rachel is already there, with a couple of American expatriates, Sue and Kip, each of whom has a house in Umbria; they've come down just for the Palio, at Dario's encouragement. I realize that these are likely the people I'd have been seated with at the contrada dinner, and suddenly it seems like I've salvaged perhaps a little of that loss. I don't even mind that I'm once again spending a whole night chatting with Americans; after the long, dreary day I've had, I'm happy to be talking to anyone.

We move on to dinner at the village's very fine restaurant, Osteria L'Antico Detto, run by an inimitable woman named

Giovanna, who talks so fast you wonder where she fits a breath in. The meal is very fine (I have a wild boar pasta), and a bottle of wine boosts our spirits; and at a certain point Dario turns to me and says, "If you wish to see a Caterpillar victory tomorrow, Rob, you should make some offering to the fates to secure it."

"What do you mean?" I ask.

"Promise to make some sacrifice or undertake some great endeavor, should the Bruco win."

"Fine, as long as it doesn't involve slicing any more bread. Take a look at that blister," I add, displaying my wounded hand to Sue, who is gracious enough to feign keen interest.

"No, seriously," Dario insists. "You ought to do it."

It's becoming clear that he's in earnest about this. "Do . . . what, exactly? What kind of thing are we talking about?"

He considers this a moment. "Well, you can make a vow that, if the contrada is victorious, you will walk from Vagliagli to Siena."

"I could do that!" I exclaim. "Wait . . . how far is that exactly?"

"Does it matter?"

"No, I'm just curious."

He extends his wineglass across the table. "Be bold. Just make the vow."

I take up my own glass and clang it against his; the resultant tone is as resonant as a gong. *"Lo giuro,"* I say. "I swear it. If the Bruco wins tomorrow, I'll walk from Vagliagli to Siena."

And just like that, I'm bound by oath.

DARK HORSE

. . .

THE NEXT DAY, I GET BACK TO MY ROOM AT THE SAN Francesco in time to shower, shave, and change clothes. Then I head out to the Società, hoping to get a glimpse of Dario—he's being done up in medieval dress, as he'll be marching in the four-hour historical procession that precedes the Palio. But the place is so thick with brucaioli, I can barely get through the door.

The entire city seems to have shifted into a different mode of existence; everything's sharper, more vibrant, more urgent. The streets are almost choked with people, but no one is lingering, no one strolls; everyone is in breathless motion, zinging about like electrons. It's almost a relief when I return to Enoteca I Terzi for lunch with Rachel, Sue, and Kip. Again: spending time with Americans. But I'm discovering to my dismay that getting close to the Sienese is more difficult than I'd ever thought, especially today. There's something about them that's almost radioactive. When they look straight at you, their eyes burn a hole in your skull.

Yet there's a lightness to the atmosphere, a kind of high fluttering in the air. Expectation is tinged with joy; these people are hair trigger today, sure, but not in the way that might snap into violence. It's more as though they're on the brink of some kind of rapturous communion—like a citywide flash mob.

Lunch is perfect; in atonement for the richness of last night's feast, I have a simple plate of linguine dressed with an arugula pesto—and of course a glass of wine, to fortify myself for the ordeal ahead. Because though my American friends have all got seats in the bleachers, I've chosen this year to watch the race as the natives do: from the teeming, swarming mass in the actual Campo.

My idea is to locate the spot where the Caterpillars are congregated and join them. In theory this should be easy enough; all I have to do is look for the blue, green, and gold fazzoletti around their necks. But once I get into the crowd, the various colors of all the various contrade merge into a kind of pointillist smear. Occasionally I think I spot a cluster of brucaioli at a distance; but when I reach the spot at which I saw them, they've dissolved, like a mirage. Finally I do come upon a large grouping—but they're all twentysomethings, more than half my age. I feel ridiculous intruding on them this way, so I melt back into the crowd, once more a man alone in a multitude. (Later I'll learn that many of the adults in the contrada don't watch the race at all; it's just too much for them. They linger in the streets and fret and worry and pray and wait for word of the result to reach them—or pace the portico of the Duomo, biting their nails, their heads hung low.)

A sudden wave of quietude sweeps over the crowd—a stirring of alertness. This must mean it's time for the members of the Carabinieri to initiate the day's proceedings with their traditional circuit of the track. The people obviously love this because they erupt in cheers when the impeccably tailored police officers (in uniforms designed by Giorgio Armani) trot out and take a lap in high-stepping dressage style—after which they launch into a furious gallop, swords drawn before them. The sheer speed drives the crowd into a frenzy. But today, something happens; the daredevil velocity claims a victim. A horse falls—within minutes, word sweeps through the crowd that it's broken its leg. (Later we'll learn that his rider only narrowly escaped being impaled on his own sword.) It's very, very seldom—in fact, it's a statistical rarity—that a horse of any kind is injured in any part of the Palio celebrations. Instantly I think to myself, Quattro Verdi. Another in the string of misfortunes.

The horse will have to be destroyed, but there seems no question of doing so in front of these assembled thousands. A truck is called in to haul the poor beast away to its doom. During the time it takes the vehicle to arrive, there's a pall over the crowd—or most of us, anyway. To my astonishment, a few dozen people raise their cellphones over their heads, to snap photos of the horse in its agony. This makes me nearly dizzy with rage; all I can do, to balance the scales, is to turn my back on the whole scene—to give the creature, to the small extent I can, his final few moments of dignity.

When the track is at long last cleared again, a gust of wind comes up and stirs the hair and collars of those of us standing in the piazza. It's as though Fate is telling us that the curse of the Quattro Verdi is sufficiently fulfilled and the Palio may proceed without incident.

The historical procession begins. As a brass band plays and the bell in the Torre del Mangia peals endlessly, each of the contrade sends out a delegation in medieval dress, including two alfieri to perform dizzying feats of daring with their contrada's banners—twirling them, leaping over them, tossing them high in the air and catching them with a single hand behind their backs. (It's the alfieri who are chiefly responsible for winning the award for most elegant contrada.) The fantino is there as well, on horseback, heroically garbed; and his mount for the race follows, led by the barbaresco. After all seventeen contrade have entered the piazza, they're followed by other delegations, including a small one representing ancient contrade that are now extinct (including the Lion, the Viper, the Bear, the Strong Sword, the Oak, and the Rooster). The procession concludes with an ox-drawn cart on which is mounted the drappellone, the Palio banner—which, in this case, is a highly stylized depiction of the track (designed by one Mario Ceroli) with the Palazzo Pubblico in the background; the earth is shown as stark white, and a herd of riderless black horses thunders around its curve—while silhouetted arms reach up toward them in ecstasy. The Madonna and Child loom over all, flanked by a star field of the racing contrade's symbols. It's undeniably striking, but I wonder if I'm the only one who notices the horses are running the wrong way: counterclockwise instead of clockwise.

When viewed from the bleachers, the procession is spectacular; it's less so, I now discover, from the interior of the Campo. The gently scalloped expanse of stone beneath us allows the crowd easily to see horses and riders who pass on the perimeter, but people marching on their own power are often obscured. I see the various banners fly into the air, but not the alfieri who hurl them, and I never do spot Dario.

The procession also moves at a very slow pace—I won't call it a crawl, but the word does flit across my mind now and then as I work to hold my stance in the overpowering heat. During the four hours that the procession requires, the sun slowly recedes, so that the area of available shade on the Campo increases, allowing the crowd to expand just a bit; but in these sardinelike conditions, even that very little is an inexpressible relief.

The fantini ride out from the Palazzo Pubblico, and whatever reaction the crowd has given up to now pales before the uproar of excitement and delight. Each jockey pauses at the gate to take a *nerbo*—the traditional riding crop made, so I understand, from dried calf's penis—and then proceeds to the starting line, the *mossa*. Here they're assigned the order in which they must line up, from the inside of the track on out: the Panther, Ram, Goose, Tower, Shell, Forest, Caterpillar, Tortoise, Eagle, and finally Dragon—this last assignment being the *rincorsa,* which is considered the worst position from the standpoint of winning but which carries with it a signal advantage. The race doesn't begin until the rincorsa approaches the mossa, so he can hold off until his ally is well situated—or his enemy poorly so.

The lineup at the mossa always takes a hellaciously long time, as unlike at traditional racetracks, here there are no starting compartments that separate the horses from their immediate neighbors. They have to align themselves on their own, and there's jostling, bumping, falling out of line—and, inevitably, several fantini break away for furtive last-minute consultations with the rincorsa and with one another, negotiating, exchanging offers, making promises. They can't be too blatant about it, of course, though everybody knows that's what's going on; some degree of stealth must be observed, or the crowd will get ugly—this being theater as much as anything else.

On this particular occasion, the entire process takes a nerve-shattering length of time—more than an hour and a half of failed attempts to draw up in formation—and in fact there are *three* separate false starts. The crowd around me is shrieking its frustration; every time the riders abandon an attempt to line up and drop back from the mossa, there's a murderous groan and threats and invective hurled across the length of the Campo that I'm actually glad I don't understand.

But eventually—finally—there's a moment of perfect accord; the Dragon breaks into a gallop; the mossa drops; the horses burst into motion, and a sound that isn't even human rises up from the piazza; it's as if suddenly the entire planet is made of hornets. All the air in the Campo, which had seemed so compressed, now explodes, like a burst balloon.

The riders are virtually flying; it's hard to keep a fix on them—like trying to watch the wind. The Goose, the Dragon, the Ram, and the Panther immediately take the first four spots, with the Caterpillar lost in the clot of those trailing behind. Then at the turn called the Casato, the fantino of the Dragon is hurled from his horse. Never mind—the horse can still win without him and appears actually capable of doing so, as it moves into second place after the Goose—and holds steady into the second lap. But hey—who's that behind him? . . . Green . . . blue . . . gold . . . it's Gingillo and Elisir for the Caterpillar! Where'd they come from? Never mind, we're suddenly in third place! No, hold on a minute—there's another bit of shuffling at San Martino—I can't really see what's going on—and by the time I get a decent view again,

Caterpillar is right on Goose's tail. This is turning out to be a *race*.

Third lap—Goose holds on to its lead; but Caterpillar creeps up—doggedly—unrelentingly—

My head is jarred by someone screaming. I realize it's me.

Caterpillar is in the lead—*widening* its lead—

—and then there's the cannon. Humanity flows over the barricades, and Gingillo and Elisir are swarmed by a mob of screaming, sobbing, ecastatic hysterics.

Everywhere I turn, people are shouting "*Bruco! Bruco! Bruco!*"

Defying every expectation and any conceivable hope, *the Caterpillar has won.*

This is the kind of upset that deranges a crowd—people will be talking about it for decades. Everyone is surging around, screaming some observation or exclamation or, I don't know, just *screaming*—and when I turn to look to where the drappellone is hung, there's already a scaffold of live brucaioli cobbled together to take it down.

This is *real*—for all its formality and tradition and the arcana of rules and protocols adhering to it, it is at its core an outlet for human passion; and for that reason it can be as dangerous as it is exalting (in fact, I don't think it's possible to be the latter *without* the former). I'm reminded of this anew, as the section of the crowd in which I'm standing decides, by some act of volition-by-gestalt, to move toward one of the arches. Individual will is neither consulted nor respected, and any attempt to resist would be not only useless but almost certainly harmful. All I can do is submit, and even then there's one terrifying moment when—as outside the Duomo five years ago—my feet are actually lifted from the ground and I'm physically carried for a space of some four yards.

Once we're through the bottleneck, the squeeze relaxes and I'm able to shimmy to the perimeter of the crowd and from there make my way—slowly, almost incrementally—to Via del Comune. The bell of the Caterpillar chapel—where earlier today Elisir was blessed and, according to tradition, told to "Go, and return victorious!"—clangs so frantically, it might just achieve escape velocity and go rocketing into the stratosphere. All up and down the street, drums beat out a staccato rhythm of euphoria. Songs splash forth from every direction, along with triumphant cries of *"Bru-bru-bruco!"* A multitude of Caterpillar banners waves up and down the street, like birds of prey swooping over a river. Light is everywhere—it's as though this little street has been over-looked by a careless nightfall.

I press my way into the Società; the garden is like some-thing out of a silent movie about the bacchanals of ancient Rome. Wine runs beneath my feet; it stains my shoes. Its musk fills the air; it's like breathing happiness. I find myself stuck for a moment, face to face with an unfamiliar visage, and I break the ice by repeating the same line the girl Beatrice used on me in 2003: "Now we are up everybody's ass!" Fortu-nately, he laughs.

By sheer luck I find Rachel, Sue, and Kip—no, no, it isn't by luck—there's no luck tonight; everything is destiny. And as if to prove it, Dario finds us as well—he's still in his medieval togs, and his green leggings are spotted with Sangiovese. When he sees us, his face contorts with emotion—the only time I've ever seen his invincible composure slip. "Can you believe it?"

he asks in a tone of voice that suggests he still can't. "We won! We won!" And then he bursts into tears.

I feel a sudden welling of joy in my own throat that threatens to reduce me to similar waterworks—but is suppressed at the last moment by a sudden epiphany: *Oh, my God. I've got to walk from Vagliagli to Siena.* When I made that vow, I hadn't thought there was a chance in Hell I'd actually have to *make good* on it.

What follows is a kind of blur. The next day, only single images will remain: leaning out the third-floor window of Società L'Alba with Rachel, watching the brucaioli below whirl and spin, as though doing a kind of dervish dance; taking my turn in the belfry, pulling the cord to sound the bell; standing back on the Campo, now scarlet in the starlight, where the pages are parading the drappellone around the piazza, the authenticity of their medieval garb betrayed by the pacifiers jutting from their lips. They're reborn; we're all reborn. It feels like an entirely new world.

THE NEXT MORNING, I join Dario and Rachel in following the Caterpillar's procession around the city, as it carries the drappellone to the other contrade to receive their congratulations. There's singing, flag waving, drumming, and a huge press of people in the streets, either spectating or marching behind. We pass several newsstands, all of which display the local paper's front page and its headline, SORPRESONA!

At each stop along the route, the Caterpillar alfieri exchange banners with their counterparts in the contrada being visited, and a display of flag tossing ensues; then the drappellone is brought inside the friendly contrada's chapel and a Te

Deum is sung. This goes on all day; we follow as long as we can, till hunger lures us away.

After a leisurely lunch at a Neapolitan tavern—salmon, crab cakes, white anchovies, linquine with mussels—we can't smile anymore, can't talk anymore. My friends return to Vagliagli; I stumble back to the San Francesco. We'll meet again in several hours, in the Società, where the three of us are on kitchen duty for the postvictory dinner.

But Dario calls later to say the dinner's been canceled due to the sudden death of the honorary rector, Luigi Socini Guelfi, who was over a hundred; he'd been captain during the legendary 1955 Palio. Instead, the entire Caterpillar contrada has been invited to dine at the Tower, which wishes to thank us for having humiliated its rival the Goose (in the Palio, finishing second is far, far worse than coming in last).

Dario, however, is taking the reprieve from kitchen duty as a chance to sleep off the excitement of the past twenty-four hours; but he urges me to attend the dinner. "The Tower is the closest of our allies; we've had many dinners together to celebrate our common victories. For instance, in 2005 we won the July Palio with Berio and Trecciolino, then they won the August Palio with Berio and Trecciolino." He has a few other examples for me, but my head is too addled to take them in.

And I do go to the Tower. But reality—which seemed to have so remarkably realigned itself last night—has clicked back into place. I may be emotionally invested in the success of the Caterpillar, but it's the investment of an observer, not a participant; and milling among the brucaioli and *torraioli,* I feel like that one guest at every wedding who doesn't fit in at any table. I'm also pretty wiped out myself, after the last day's roller-coaster ride. So after a quick bite I slip quietly away.

I'm not dissatisfied with this adventure; how can I be? An upset of the kind I witnessed yesterday would be thrilling under any circumstances; but it was a Caterpillar victory into the bargain. I was able to watch as Gingillo was transformed from a nobody into a legend, carried atop the shoulders of the contrada he'd just propelled to the apex of the Sienese hierarchy. I got to witness the triumphant performance of a heroic steed named Elisir, in whom no one had placed any hope.

But I'm no closer to the brucaioli now than I was when I started. And I can see how it would be impossible to have come away from this experience otherwise; this is the climax of their social year, and they had a horse and rider in the thick of it. Next August, they won't. They'll have no stakes in the race; their concentration will be less fierce, their focus less impenetrable. It might make sense to come back then and try again.

And in fact, I *have* to come back. I'm obliged to fulfill my vow to the fates, to walk from Vagliagli to Siena.

But for now I must take my leave. As I go, I resist the urge to wave. No one will see it; no one's looking my way.

~

AFTER I'VE BEEN HOME a few weeks, I get an email from Dario, telling me that he's just come from the rescheduled *cena della prova generale*—the Palio-eve dinner that had been rained out. The whole event was conducted as though it had occurred on the night it should have—as though the Palio had not yet been run. "We know we haven't got a chance," the rector Fabio said in his speech; "we know the horse isn't capable of winning. Let's just enjoy tomorrow as much as we can."

If I needed further reminding why I love these people, that would've done it.

PART THREE

Summer · 2009

. . .

The

DEBUTANTS

Out of POCKET

. . .

⯘ IT'S BEEN A LONG FLIGHT, AND I'M EAGER TO HAVE IT done, but as we circle over Florence the pilot announces that due to a backup on the runways below, we're being diverted to Pisa. Groans of exasperation—my own among them. But he assures us that there will be buses waiting outside the airport to take us to Florence.

By this time I'm familiar enough with Italy and the Italians to know that when they say there'll be buses waiting outside the airport, there won't be any such thing for at least two hours. And part of me wonders whether I shouldn't just bolt. I can as easily reach Siena from Pisa as I can from Florence.

Except . . . it *will* be very late by the time we touch down. And I do have a hotel reservation in Florence, and it would be a lot easier to arrive in Siena tomorrow, fresh and ready, than to straggle into town in the dead of night, with no one expecting me and nowhere to go.

So I decide to wait for the buses, which, just as I said, are nowhere to be found. Neither is anyone from the airline around to help us out. A little clutch of the more type-A passengers, refusing to accept that this is the case, circumnavigate the parking lot, asking the driver of every bus on the premises

whether *he's* the one commissioned to take the diverted ar-
rivals to Florence, though it's perfectly apparent to the rest of
us that none of them is.

I've come back this year with higher hopes of connecting
with the Caterpillar crowd. It's Palio time again, and everyone
will still be high on their victory of last August; but I'm
counting on their being slightly less frenetic, less distracted,
because this time they're not running. (There was a chance
they'd be drawn to fill one of the three open slots in the race,
but they weren't, so they're sitting this one out.)

That doesn't mean they won't be actively involved. The
Giraffe is running, and though officially there is no longer a
rivalry between that contrada and the Caterpillar, no one in
the Bruco will want to see it win. Whereas Tower and Porcupine, both allies of the Bruco, are running as well, and the
brucaioli will do what they can, behind the scenes, to help
them; though the rumor is that the Porcupine doesn't want to
win. It's still paying off its victory of last July. That's the
downside of winning a Palio; it's *expensive.*

And then there's the Owl; it hasn't had a victory in
thirty years. Almost everyone would find an Owl victory
satisfying—except, of course, its bitter rival, the Unicorn,
which is also racing; but rather than focusing on its own
chances, the Unicorn's main objective will be to stop the Owl,
keeping it firmly in the humiliating "grandmother" spot (i.e.,
the contrada with the longest losing streak).

I have plenty of time to ruminate on all this as I stroll the
length of the Pisa airport, waiting for the bus to arrive. It
shows up after only about fifty minutes—which for Italians is
downright alacrity—and I find a nice, comfortable window

seat and sink into it. In fact, it's so cozy—and the hum of the motor so soothing—that I drop right off to sleep and don't awaken till the bus pulls up in front of Florence's Peretola Airport and brakes with a brain-shattering hiss.

I stagger out, collect my bag from the luggage compartment, and hail a cab. I throw my bag into its trunk, then get in and direct the driver to take me to the center of town.

He pulls away and heads toward the ramp leading to the highway. As he does so, I reach into my pocket for my wallet. It's one of my little quirks; I like to have the fare all tallied up and ready before I actually arrive at my destination.

But my wallet isn't in my pocket.

It isn't in my other pocket either.

It isn't in my back pockets, or any of the pouches on my carry-on, or—anywhere. My wallet isn't *anywhere*.

I lean forward and tell the driver—in a voice I immediately recognize as too frantic, too high-pitched—to pull over, pull over, something's wrong.

While he's parked on the side of the road I spastically grope myself all over a few more times, hoping for a telltale bulge—where? over my shoulder blade? inside my sock? am I crazy?—but there's nothing, nothing, nothing.

"I have to get out," I tell him. "I can't pay you." He says something to me in return that I don't catch, but I'm in no condition even to try to understand. I fumble my way out of the cab and slam the door, and he drives away.

With my bag in his trunk.

It takes me a few seconds to realize this; then I give chase, shouting and flailing my arms—but it's no use. His taillights grow smaller and dimmer, and then he's gone.

And I'm standing on the side of a road in a strange country in the middle of the night, with no cash, no credit cards, no change of clothing, no toothbrush, no *anything*.

Actually, that's not quite true; I do have my cellphone and my passport, both of which were tucked into the opposite pocket from the one that bore the wallet. Which, I now realize, was very likely stolen—plucked from my hip while I was, what? Looking the opposite direction? Talking to a fellow passenger?—I try to recall whether anyone bumped into me, grazed me; and if so, where. But it's impossible to know for sure; over the past several hours I've been through two airports and aboard a bus, and asleep for some of it. Someone pressing against me, or touching me, wouldn't be even remotely worth noting.

But there's a chance that the wallet *wasn't* stolen—that it fell out of my pocket on the bus. Accordingly I run all the way back to the terminal, hoping to catch the bus before it departs—only to have it nearly mow me down as it barrels away from the terminal. I actually have to leap out of its path to avoid being killed, landing on the side of the road and skidding across some gravel into something that makes a disquieting squish.

I get unsteadily to my feet and dust myself off, then head inside to clean up at the public restroom. And it's only then, staring at my pale, wild-eyed face in the mirror, that I realize how deep is the shit in which I now am. The airport is a ghost town at this late hour. All the kiosks and counters are shuttered; there doesn't appear even to be an official of any kind on-site.

Back out in the terminal, I plonk myself into a chair, phone in hand. The charge is almost gone, so I have to choose carefully whom I dial. I had, before leaving, jotted down all my credit card numbers in case they were lost or stolen; but I did that in a small moleskin notebook that I tucked into my carry-on bag, which is now in the back of a cab whose license plate and number I didn't have a chance to note. The only alternative left is to call Jeffrey in Chicago and tell him—in a tone of voice I try to keep steady and rational, though with apparently limited success because he keeps telling me to "Calm down"—to go to my file drawer and get all my credit records and call in the missing cards for me. I don't even know what time it is in America, but it doesn't matter—it's already a pretty big imposition; the kind that really tests relationships. He promises to handle it, and while we're talking the call waiting alert starts booping. It's Dario, checking to see whether I've landed safely. Yes, I tell him, I've *landed* safely; but now I'm stuck at the Florence airport and will have to survive the coming days by eating the remains of discarded off-brand Euro-snacks that I scavenge from trash bins.

Suddenly Dario, too, is telling me to calm down. In the kind of voice you'd use on an idiot child or an easily distracted dog, he tells me to take a cab to Florence and have the desk manager advance me the fare; then tomorrow Dario will send someone to pick me up and settle my bill. It's an eminently reasonable and kind solution, though he has to repeat it in its entirety because in my present state of mind it sounds like a geometric theorem in Urdu.

Just having someone looking out for me—someone actually on the same continent, no less—has a calming effect, and I'm able to go back outside to the taxi stand with some degree of equanimity. It's very late, and there aren't many cabs to be had—but there's one just pulling away from the curb. I recognize the driver; it's the guy who picked me up twenty minutes ago. He must've just circled back to get another fare.

Once again I find myself chasing him down, and when he pauses at a speed bump I hammer my fists on his trunk. He sticks his head out the window and stares at me with eyes so wide they look like they're attached to novelty glasses, as I tell him in a mixture of English, Italian, and Crazy Person that my bag is in his trunk. Eventually I persuade him to pop it open so I can retrieve it, after which he peels away as though afraid I might now climb up on his hood and start humping his windshield.

The two remaining taxi drivers, having witnessed all this, are equally reluctant to have me in their backseat, especially when I explain that I have no actual cash. But eventually, by some means, I persuade one of them and he drives me to Florence, where the hotel, having been alerted by Dario, checks me into a room with minimal explanation on my part.

Now that I've got my bag back, I have access to all my records, so I call American Express—which has already canceled my card, thanks to Jeffrey—and ask for a cash advance on my account. The people there are perfectly obliging, and ask how much I want; I say, "Nine hundred dollars," and they don't even balk, which makes me feel like I'm such a tremendously savvy traveler, massaging victory from the mire of defeat.

But then the representative says she has to ask a few "security questions" to ascertain that I am indeed me. Purely a formality. The questions include: What is the square footage of your house? What was your last zip code? And what was your last telephone number?

I'm not able to answer any of them. I mean, come on. I've

lived in my house for thirteen years, I don't remember my last zip code or phone number. I can barely remember the name of the guy across the hall. As for my square footage—are you goddamn kidding me? "Do you know the square footage of *your* house?" I ask the representative. She says, "Mr. Rodi, these questions are chosen because they're a matter of public record," and it's here that I lose my cool pretty much completely. "If they're a matter of public record," I howl, "then *why are you using them as security questions?*" I'm so mad I actually jump up and down, like an anime character.

The upshot is, I'm declined. American Express will advance me exactly zilch. I don't remember exactly what I say after that; I do recall that the language was more than usually colorful. It's probably all transcribed in my permanent record somewhere.

Still, if my permanent record meant anything, I'd have been taken out and shot years ago.

*T*AGALONG

. . .

⚜ I HAVE NO BETTER LUCK WITH AMERICAN EXPRESS THE next day. The best they can do is to send a replacement card, which won't reach me till I'm actually leaving Italy; in fact, it will be delivered to my hotel here in Florence the night before I fly home.

I'm somewhat more sanguine about all this now that I've had a good night's sleep. The problem I now have is that I've lost my independence. Since I have no cash and no means of getting any, I'll be completely reliant on Dario—to the extent that I won't be able to go my own way in Siena. It doesn't hurt my pride—that being a battered old tank that's taken too many hits to care anymore—but it does mean I'm far less able to make any impression on the brucaioli beyond the one they already have of me: Dario's American friend. It won't make for a wasted visit, but it might mean many missed opportunities.

A car arrives for me at the hotel, and its driver—a Roman transplant named Sandro whom Dario has trained as a Chianti tour guide—pays my bill using Dario's credit card, then speeds me off to Siena. He's an affable enough fellow, but no fan of either the Palio (too "brutal") or the contrade ("arrogant"). This is something of an epiphany for me, because if you take "brutal" and "arrogant" and give them just the slightest twist, the light glints off them differently, and what you get are "fierce" and "passionate," which are two of the attributes that have brought me back here, like a lovesick suitor. One man's grease and sugar paste is another man's Twinkies.

Dario texts me to meet him on the Campo, at Bar Palio, where he's escorting a couple from New Zealand, the Meads, to the extraction of the horses. I feel terrible about having to barge in on them this way; after all, they've paid handsomely for Dario's time, and now I'm intruding on it. But as it happens they recognize my name from Dario's books and are delighted to have me along. It's my first indication that Dario has become, for some people, almost as enticing a phenomenon as the Palio itself, and they relish inside glimpses into his exotic life and international connections. They're very gracious, at any rate, and pretend to be riveted by the story of my lost wallet. So much so that it takes a few moments for Dario to get us all back on track and finish his rundown of the current state of Palio politics.

This particular race, we learn, has been dubbed *il Palio dei debuttanti*—the Palio of the Debutants—because there are a whopping six new horses, with only four returning veterans. (I ask about Elisir, but alas, he won't be back; he recently suffered a slight injury that has removed him from competition. But you can't feel bad for him; according to the protocols instituted by the city of Siena, any horse who has ever run a Palio is entitled to retire to a *pensionario* where he can spend the rest of his days running free.) This sheer number of debuting horses makes it more difficult to handicap the various contrade's chances. But it may give a slight edge to the contrade who have gone the longest without a victory and who are therefore presumably richer (never having had to pay out for a win).

After I've inhaled all the chips and pretzels on the table (it's the first food I've had since the plane), we head into the Campo to watch the extraction. It's lacking a little in its usual drama—with so many new horses, it's less clear which contrada walks away with the advantage—but it's always a thrill to witness the complete immersion of the crowd in the procedure. There's something uncanny about an assemblage some thousand persons strong, maintaining a silence so complete you can practically hear the anxious grinding of teeth.

I haven't really stopped to take my bearings till now; everything since I landed has been so unmoored. But now, standing in the Campo, with the long shadow of the Torre del Mangia falling over the gathering as though collecting us all into an embrace—and the intense focus of those around me, their utter fixation on the activities of the officials seated on the platform before the Palazzo Pubblico as they draw first the name of the horse, then that of the contrada whose hopes will literally ride on its back—all this provokes in me a stillness of equal ardor. And I feel at once a sudden pull, an involuntary but welcome lapsing into something, not quite eternal but of such uncanny reliability that it might be considered as inevitable as the seasons, as the phases of the moon: *i giorni del Palio*—the days of the Palio. A great ongoing narrative that is always new and always the same; always fraught with the unexpected, yet reliable in its familiarity. I find myself so much more present in this single moment, so highly aware of its place in both the context of what has led up to it and what will launch forth from it, that petty concerns such as lost wallets fade into silly insignificance. I barely notice the heat of the day, the way the sun prickles the skin over my scalp and my shirt clings damply to my back; I'm too gripped by events—by the power of story.

Afterward, when the mounts have all been assigned, Dario takes the Meads to a prearranged lunch at La Compagnia dei Vinattieri, a Caterpillar-owned restaurant in the Goose contrada. I am, of course, compelled to tag along due to my inability to feed myself. The conversation dwells principally on the mechanics of the Palio—this is, after all, why the Meads enlisted Dario to accompany them in the first place—though later we're all introduced to the proprietor, a surprisingly youthful gent named Marco; and there he is, another brucaiolo under my belt.

After the meal, with the Meads deposited back at their hotel (the exceptionally beautiful Palazzo Ravizza), Dario— knowing that I'm eager to reconnect with the life of the contrada—takes me to Società L'Alba, where a number of brucaioli linger congenially in the garden. We amble up to the bar and have a prosecco; it goes quickly, so we have another. I'm still lugging my baggage behind me, which must mark me as an interloper in the eyes of everyone who speaks to us, but they're cordial enough, and I'm really, honestly beginning to unclench.

We drive to Dario's village of Vagliagli, where we spot a friend of his, Clara, outside Bar San Cristoforo. The old woman, her age-defying vanity betrayed by her full makeup and jaunty hat, stops to talk through the car window, basically ignoring me until she hears that I'm a friend and neighbor of Rachel, at which time I become a person of great interest to her. She entrusts me to take her love to Rachel—

she uses what I presume is an idiomatic expression, something like "Carry her my love in your pocket," which makes me reflect momentarily how unsafe my pockets have lately proven—and when I look up again, I find her crying. Rachel has clearly made a conquest here, and more resoundingly than I've been able to manage in my own time in Tuscany.

Since we're right at Bar San Cristoforo, we figure we might as well stop. I say hello to Maria the proprietress, who beams a welcoming smile at me, as though I've been away only a few days. We order another round of prosecchi and sit outside under the canopy, where, perhaps inevitably, we fall into conversation with two English-speaking German tourists, middle-aged professional men who recognize Dario from his author photos and can scarcely believe their good luck at running into him (I am merely a bonus). I begin to understand my role in Dario's public image: I'm the wacky sidekick. I'm Rhoda Morgenstern.

Dario's friend Michele stops by as well, and since he speaks only Italian he and I converse while Dario entertains his fans. Michele insists on buying me another drink, and I'm reminded that the days of the Palio can become marathons of alcohol consumption if you're not careful. I've been far from careful today but make a vow to do better tomorrow.

Back at Dario's house, there's one last glass of wine as we watch the exclusive victory DVD the Caterpillar produced after last year's unexpected triumph. Most notable is a section at the end, in which brief scenes of very old brucaioli are intercut with those of the young children of the contrada, all of them saying the same thing: "In my life I have seen three victories." It's a funny, sweet way of dramatizing the difference between the culo and sfiga generations—and how different the emotional lives of these children will be from those of their long-parched but ever hopeful elders.

As I drift off to sleep, it occurs to me: I myself have seen *two* victories. And suddenly, never mind my wallet, I feel lucky again.

A LOT of CHIANTI, a LITTLE ROSÉ

...

ALL THE NEXT DAY I AM, BY NECESSITY, DARIO'S WINGMAN. I accompany him to the magnificent hotel in the Chianti countryside, Relais Borgo Scopeto, where he meets the Meads for lunch. They seem genuinely pleased to see me again, so I feel obligated to give them my full attention—though I'm temporarily distracted by the sight of Vanessa Redgrave sailing across the courtyard. Dario explains that a movie, *Letters to Juliet,* has just finished filming in the area and that the cast are accommodated here. I've been dazzled by Redgrave since she was a kooky sixties gamine in *Morgan!,* so it's hard for me to take my eyes off her. She's an old woman now, but I'm still left with a sense of almost spiritual elation, as though Aphrodite had crossed my path, or Titania, or the Lady of the Lake.

After lunch, we leave the Meads in the charge of one of Dario's lieutenants and head back to Siena, where we soon find ourselves at Bar Macario downing Tuscan beer. It feels as though I never left; the place is as jammed with brucaioli as ever, and the talk is all Palio, Palio, Palio—though with less urgency now, since the Caterpillar isn't *in corsa,* as they say.

After our thirst is quenched, we head down Via dei Rossi on our way to Società L'Alba but are waylaid by Luigina, who's having a drink at the little bar just two doors down from the San Francesco, where I stayed last year. I recall looking out my window at this place—which appears, intriguingly, to have no discernible identity (all it says on the door is "Caffetteria, Sala da Tè," which is a description, not a name). Its little two-table patio is the scene of a continuous coming and going of brucaioli, who meet singly or in small parties, linger, talk, drink, smoke, and move on. It seems scarcely credible that I'm now taking a seat here myself; I feel as though I've just passed some invisible velvet rope.

In the Sienese way, we're joined by several others as they pass, some of whose acquaintance I make, others of whom don't pause long enough for an introduction. One of the more memorable is Giuliano Ghiselli, a silver-haired fox with ice blue eyes and an edge to his voice that would stop traffic, if cars were allowed on these streets. He has tremendous natural authority and in fact plenty of institutional authority as well; he's a writer, lecturer, TV personality, and general expert on this city and its history. Possibly he's a resource I can tap later. He also appears to be someone who doesn't suffer fools gladly.

Then on to a dinner at Società; and again there's the feeling of never having left. The garden seems to have existed in a state of enchanted immutability since I was here last: everything is just as I last saw it—the lights, the textures, the gentle lapping of conversation against shores of song. The only difference is that no one tonight is wearing a fazzoletto. As Dario explains it, that's done only during times when the contrada is in corsa.

During the dinner I meet Peggy Castaldi, an American woman from San Francisco who now lives here part-time and who's actually been baptized in the contrada. She's bright and funny, with a cascade of impossibly abundant auburn hair, and seems to mesh seamlessly with the natives; I ask her what her secret is, and she looks at me oddly. "Just being here," she says, as if *obviously* that's all it takes; and I can see that it might be all it takes *her.* Some people are like open windows; there's no artifice, no expectation, no apprehension in them—they joyfully embrace any new experience. I'm not an open window, not even a shuttered one. I feel more like the trapdoor to the cellar with the padlock that's rusted shut. Got to get a crowbar and pry that baby open. I'm trying, I'm trying, but I'm a different order of human being from people like Peggy and Rachel, and before them Roy Moskovitz. But that doesn't mean I can't learn. And these are the people I've selected to teach me, right here, right now.

After dinner we stop in the kitchen to volunteer ourselves for tomorrow's big event: the *cena della prova generale*. I recognize a few of the staff and stop to say hello; then we depart the Bruco—but not for home. Dario has an appointment in the Pantera (Panther) contrada, where he's arranged to pick up bleacher tickets for the Meads. I accompany him—basically, I'm afraid to let him out of my sight, given my current pauperism. The Panther—not so large nor so rich a contrada as the Caterpillar—has its dinners in the lobby of a movie theater. But its residents' ebullience is undeniable; there's no shortage of joy here.

Dario leaves me in the care of one of the contrada's *provicari,* Filippo, while he conducts his transaction. A very boyish fortysomething, Filippo is only too happy to treat me to a drink and answer my questions about life in the Panther. In fact, I almost get the impression that I'm being courted—that my affiliation with the Bruco represents a challenge to this son of the Panther. Possibly I'm imagining things; possibly my difficulty in breaking through the reserve of the brucaioli is making me wonder whether my devotion would be more gladly received *here*. Possibly I'm just drunk. Actually, scratch that "possibly." In the end I remain true to the Caterpillar, though with a new sense of fraternal affection for the Panther. I will be its earnest advocate in any endeavor in which it's not in direct competition with the Bruco. As I'm sure they appreciate.

The next night we arrive early to undertake our duties for the big Palio-eve cena. Fortunately, this time I'm not buried away in the sweltering kitchen but am out on the patio, manning the wine table with Dario. The contrada supplies plenty of free table wine, but those who prefer a more complex vintage can come to us and buy a nice bottle of Lamole di Lamole Chianti Classico. This turns out to be a much more felicitous assignment; for one thing, it's a pleasant night with a slight hint of breeze, so my sweating stays within a range generally considered normal for inhabitants of this planet; and also, I get to meet dozens of brucaioli as they arrive to give us their custom. We take their cash, pull the corks for them, and have a nice chat while we're doing it.

As the free wine on the table runs out, the traffic to our table increases, and suddenly I find myself working rather harder than I'd anticipated. I'm lugging crates from the storeroom, tearing them open and uncorking them as fast as I can, and taking euros from a wall of people three deep. No one feels like chatting now. Dario has gone off for a smoke, leaving me on my own, and he's gone so long I begin to picture him puffing away on some enormous foot-long cigar. Possibly this is his way of testing me, like when you teach toddlers how to swim by just throwing them in the pool.

And swim I do. In fact, I manage to last out the evening and close up shop all by myself. This gives me time to doff my apron, have a celebratory cup of wine myself (my first of the day, thank you very much), and take my first real spin through the garden. And it's there I get a close-up view of the dinner's special guest: Rose Rosa, the horse that won the 1996 Palio that ended the Bruco's long losing streak. Earlier, she'd been given a formal introduction and a grand entrance, and at the sight of her everyone stood up and sang the song composed in her honor, "Rose Rosa la Cavallina Nostra"; and though I couldn't see this from my vantage point behind the wine table, I later heard that there were many grateful tears. The former captain, Riccardo, gave a speech in tribute during which he was visibly moved, followed by another from Gianni the vicario. This girl has got herself some serious *lauding*.

And why not? Her career is certainly laudatory. She gained her first victory (for the Unicorn) in her very first Palio, in August 1995, under the name Bella Speranza—i.e., Beautiful Hope. Perhaps thinking that her victory negated her name (the hope having been quite splendidly realized), she was rechristened Rose Rosa in time to become a legend among the Caterpillar a year later. After which she retired to a life of ease. Three consecutive Palii, two of which she won . . . not a bad lifetime average.

When I reach her, she's ambling about the stall that has been specially erected for her, seeming to glory in her celebrity. In fact, I can barely see her due to the adoring crowd around her; some parents are lifting their children high over the stall's walls to have their photos taken with her. This is one of the indelible traits of the Sienese people: they either love or hate their jockeys, but they *exalt* their horses. In fact, the brucaioli so revere Rose Rosa that the pink rose on their contrada emblem, adjacent to the image of the rampant caterpillar and its crown (denoting its noble status), is now indelibly associated with her; and in fact this bloom seems in retrospect to have been an uncanny prediction of her glorious arrival in the contrada's history.

But this devotion isn't reserved only for victorious mounts. All a horse needs do is race *one* Palio, and it's entitled to spend the rest of its days at a pensionario where, at the expense of the grateful Sienese, it's free to roam and run the meadows to its heart's content (which, as I noted earlier, is the fate currently enjoyed by Elisir). For this reason, the average life span of a Palio horse is an enviable twenty-eight years.

The Sienese have also worked with animal rights groups to set up processes and protocols to prevent accidents and injuries on the track. These include selecting only half-breeds (more adept at the demands of the course than Thoroughbreds), and only between seven and ten years old—as well as instituting no-doping rules and strict veterinary supervision before and after the race. The Sienese protocols have been very successful—it's been a decade since a Palio horse was injured—and have been used as an example by animal rights groups throughout the nation.

The Florentine writer Paola Fallaci, after coming to Siena and seeing the way the horses are treated here, wrote, "If I were to be reincarnated, I would choose to be a *cavallo da Palio*." (She later amended this: "A *cavalla,* since the males are castrated.") This is, I now realize, the most significant way in which I differ from the Sienese: they're all equine enthusiasts, if not outright fanatics; connoisseurs of horseflesh, obsessed by each animal's character, traits, and abilities. My awareness of the horses has been largely peripheral; my interest is drawn instead to the workings of contrada society. This moment, right here and now, is the perfect illustration of this immutable dichotomy: all the brucaioli are gazing with wonder at Rose Rosa, while I'm gazing with wonder at the brucaioli themselves.

Soon the tables start emptying of their occupants, and a kind of protracted leave-taking begins, the final smattering of revelers moving toward the stairs to the clubhouse with glacial leisure. I collect leftover bottles from the vacated tables and take them back to the wine stand to (ssshh) consolidate their contents. Dario returns just as I'm sweeping up the litter of corks. I don't know where he's been all this time, and I'm not about to ask; as far as I'm concerned, after four days of my loping behind him like an organ grinder's monkey, he's deserved a few hours of private time.

On the way out we run into the rector, Fabio, who not only remembers me but thanks me for a job well done. Apparently, my humble labors in the corner of the garden have not gone unnoticed.

No chance of a Palio win tomorrow, true—but, just like that, it's a banner day for me.

ℵIGHT OWL

. . .

⚒ ALL THAT PHYSICAL LABOR TAKES ITS TOLL; ON THE morning of the day of the Palio, my arms and legs seem to be about three times heavier than usual, as though I've awakened on Jupiter instead of Earth.

Wait—did I say the *morning* of the day of the Palio? It's actually a little past that. In fact, Dario and I have to scramble to make it to Siena in time. Which is unfortunate, because neither one of us is quite in scrambling condition.

It's only when we've just crossed the city limits that we realize we've got several long hours in bleacher seats ahead of us and that we'd accordingly better eat something. Dario swings his van into the drive-through lane of a McDonald's and pulls up to the speaker. In the moment before it crackles to life and asks our order, he turns to me and says, with an explicit threat in his voice, "Never tell *anyone* we did this."

The bare rudiments of nutrition now attended to, we continue to the *centro storico,* where parking is so ridiculously impossible that pretty much everyone has just left their cars wherever it is they finally decided to give up. I suppose God—and the Sienese police—must give a special dispensation to scofflaws on Palio day.

We meet the Meads at Palazzo Rivizza and make our way to the Campo, doing our best to stay united in the churning sea of fazzoletti. We scuttle down a narrow alleyway, where an official takes our tickets; and then it's up, up, up to our tiny bleacher seats. They're just as uncomfortable as I recall: small and hard and without backs, and there's really no place to put your feet, and we're here for at least four hours so let's hope no one feels the call of nature, because nature can't be answered.

The carabinieri come out for their traditional charge, and the sound of hoofbeats triggers something in me; a kind of pause button on my consciousness.

The historical procession begins, and Dario offers a running commentary for the Meads. I can't help comparing this with my experience last year, standing among the masses in the piazza, striving to hold my ground while trying in vain to catch some glimpse of the marchers. Suddenly, here I am with a bird's-eye view *and* expert commentary.

The procession eventually concludes; there's a hush over the entire Campo. I know I should be feeling the thrum of expectation, but I'm distracted by my mustache, which still smells strongly of Filet-O'-Fish. An unseasonably cool breeze comes up; Mrs. Mead draws a sweater around her shoulders.

Then the fantini ride out of the Palazzo Pubblico, and everything goes TILT. Suddenly there's no weather, no odor, no uncomfortable seating—there's just *this moment,* as people call out urgently and affectionately to the men (and the horses) who carry their hopes on their backs.

The order of the lineup is announced. Giraffe is called out first and so gets the inside track. I feel a little hardening in the air around Dario when this plum position is awarded to our "invisible enemy." The Snail is called last and so will be rin-corsa. All that's left now is the race.

Going on two hours later, that's *still* all that's left. There's been an absolutely gut-wrenching mess at the mossa—a kind of equine equivalent to a can of worms—and the demeanor of the crowd has devolved from expectant to indignant. There've been a few instances when everyone got into place—and held it—and the crowd drew its collective breath in a *this-is-it* kind of way—only to have the rincorsa hold back instead of seizing the moment. The cries of *"Vai, vai, asino,"* fly over our heads like grapeshot. Three maddening false starts haven't exactly helped the mood. Dario keeps looking at the sky, which is rapidly deepening in hue. "I give it fifteen minutes," he says, "before they call the race for darkness." Which would mean postponement; which would mean starting all over again tomorrow. The Meads seem espe-cially distressed by this possibility, because they're leaving town in the morning.

I can't but reflect that it *was* a smart move to grab that fast food on our way in, whether we wanted it or not. Without it, I'd have filched Mrs. Mead's sweater right off her shoulders and started gnawing it like a side of spareribs. As it is, I keep flicking my tongue up into the recesses of my mustache, hop-ing to find a crumb or two that went astray.

I gaze up at the heavens and realize daylight has now essen-tially receded. What's left is just the ochre tinge it's left behind—embers. It won't be long before the Campo is draped in dusk. It's strange, gazing at the skies; they seem so peaceful—the waning of day is so calming, like being gath-ered into a mother's arms. Yet here below, there's only furor and frustration. Though these people aren't raging against the dying of the light so much as they are against the *mossiere,* the official responsible for dropping the mossa at the appropriate moment. Dario's ready to pull his hair out. I'm just resigning myself to the fact of a postponement . . . .

. . . when suddenly, they're off. The mossa has dropped, the riders are in corsa, and it's balls to the wall. It takes me a few moments to recover from the shock; and then—and then—well, what *is* happening out there? It's gotten so dark I can't actually see.

A whirlwind ninety seconds later, the Owl careens past the finish—poetically, since the owl is a nocturnal bird, and this is now undeniably its element; the Campo is shimmering in twilight. It's also an emotionally satisfying outcome, because with this victory, the Owl sheds its shameful role as the Palio "grandmother." The She-Wolf now assumes that title; its last victory was in 1989 (with a riderless horse). Accordingly the She-Wolf's enemy, the Porcupine, will be celebrating tonight as though they themselves had won.

The members of the Owl—the *cittevini*—are rapturous. But it's so dusky, it's left largely to the ears to discern the transports of ecstasy being enjoyed: shrieks, cries, sobs, invocations. And song. Always, always, even in their moments of greatest distraction, the Sienese find the will to sing.

MY TIME RUNS OUT; I have to go back home to America. Reluctantly, I'm forced at last to borrow cash from Dario to get myself to Florence, where I'll catch my flight early the next day. He doesn't begrudge it, of course, and I'll repay him as soon as I'm home—but still it rankles my pride. I don't like inconveniencing my friends. And to make the matter vastly more irritating, I find my replacement AmEx card waiting for me at my Florence hotel. It's not too little, but it's definitely too late.

This just exacerbates my nagging sense of unease. I'm not entirely satisfied with the time I've spent here. Oh, I've enjoyed myself, as I always do in Siena, but enjoyment isn't why I've come. The whole point of this enterprise is to immerse myself in the life of the Caterpillar contrada and with any luck be embraced by its members in return. I've made very little progress in that respect. And though I've chosen to blame this on the loss of my wallet—which left me dependent on Dario and unable to venture out on my own—I have to acknowledge that that's not really the case. I could have figured out some way to get around if I'd really tried. The problem, I now realize, was that I didn't have any idea what to do with that kind of autonomy: where to go, whom to talk to. It actually served me better to stay close to Dario, since he's a brucaiolo and knows the ropes.

And suddenly it seems clear to me, *painfully* clear, that I've been going about this the wrong way. I can't ever learn the ways of the Bruco or come to understand its character by showing up only at Palio time. July and August are periods of hyperreality for them; everything is urgent, in a state of heightened agitation—even when they're not in corsa. If I'm serious about seeing the contrada's true face, I need to be here during the rest of the year. The Palio, after all, isn't the real story; the community is. And I need to see that community shorn of its window dressing. What goes on here in fall or the dead of winter? Where does spring find the brucaioli? *Those* are the things I need to discover.

The additional benefit is that, during an ordinary week in

an average season, an American visitor to Società L'Alba might be a bit more visible. Might even, possibly, be worthy of interest.

All right, then. Home for now.

But not for long. And not entirely.

Because I'm leaving a little bit of my heart right here.

PART FOUR

Autumn · 2009

. . .

CLOSE

ENCOUNTERS

SUMMON the $H E \mathcal{R} O E S$

. . .

IT'S A CHILLY FALL AFTERNOON; I'VE JUST ARRIVED IN Siena by train, and I have several hours ahead of me with flapall to do. Looked at one way, that might mean I'm footloose and fancy free; I could go blithely leapfrogging from contrada to contrada, ducking into and out of chapels, museums, shops, and tavernas, chatting up the locals in my increasingly confident Tuscan. But alas, I'm hampered by my suitcase. I've tried to pack as lightly as possible, and in fact it's just a carryon bag, several degrees smaller than some of the backpacks I see young student types hauling on their shoulders, stooping them so low you can't tell whether they're on their way to Club Med or Calvary. But even so my bag is a burden; by the time I've wheeled it from the station to the Campo, the sound of it rattling over the cobblestones has frayed my nerves to thin silken strands.

Ideally, of course, I'd have met up with Dario on arrival and gone back to his place to freshen up and dump my luggage, but Dario's not here to provide stopover services. In fact, he's been on my home turf, the great Midwest, touring to promote both the latest pressing of his Rasna olive oil and his new memoir, *Too Much Tuscan Wine.*

He's set to return to his native soil this afternoon, and accordingly I booked my flight for the same day, so that I could avail myself again of his hospitality. What I hadn't counted on was him having a later arrival time than me—several hours later, in fact. But that's how it's worked out, and for that reason we've arranged to meet at the contrada tonight, where there's a cena scheduled—a Dinner with the Captain, one of a regular series hosted by Gianni Falciani. Tonight's event is called *Gli Assassini di Gianni*—The Assassins of Gianni, "assassins" being another term applied to the jockeys of the Palio. And in fact there's a pair of special guests scheduled: the fantini who won the last three Bruco victories, Trecciolino and Gingillo. Gingillo's father, who raced for the Caterpillar in 1972, will also be on hand, though more in the position of proud parent than special guest.

But in the meantime, I'm on my own and saddled with my suitcase—which seems to be inexplicably adding heft and weight with each mile I march.

I head for the contrada, remembering the vitality of the street life there; my hope is that I'll run into someone I know. But though a few faces do look either familiar or approachable, I'm suddenly aware of how I myself must appear, bursting unannounced onto these well-ordered thoroughfares, the wheels of my suitcase creating the kind of racket that sends flocks of pigeons into frightened flight.

So instead I take refuge on the Campo, where I won't look at all out of place, since it's inevitably crawling with tourists. It's actually good to be back there; it still strikes me as one of the loveliest, *shapeliest* public spaces in the world, with its masculine outlines softened by the feminine slope of the piazza and its forbidding wall of stone muted by rich earthen colors.

Seated at an outdoor café, I sink into a kind of temporal tor-
por; I've looked out on this vista so many times, it can feel as
though everything I've experienced outside it is just something I've daydreamed while sitting here.

Feeding this illusion is the lack of any intrusion by the natural world. There's a distinct chill in the air; autumn holds full
sway. But you'd never know it from outward appearances;
there are no trees to shed their leaves, no lawns to run brown.
The only visible indications of the season are the jackets and
hats being worn by those who've come here.

I order up a prosecco, and the waiter brings me, as an ac-
companiment, a dish of tiny sandwiches, each about the size
of a matchbox and irresistibly good. It occurs to me that more
of them may arrive if I order more prosecco. Which is in fact
the case—thus sating both my hunger and my thirst as I sit beneath the shade of the umbrella and write at length in my
notebook on the subject of how to define "homecoming"—
whether the determining factor is whether the place you've
returned to *feels* like home, or whether you have to have in
fact actually lived there.

By the time the sun has meandered low enough to warrant
a return trip to the contrada, I'm feeling pretty good even
though my brand-new wallet is distressingly lighter. There it
is, the bane of every international traveler: it's at least several
days before you can treat those pretty little leaflets as money.
Euros are especially problematic because they come in different sizes, so the smaller denominations can get tucked away
inside the larger ones; you get to the point where even if you
can't see them, you just expect them to be there. Then, later
on, you peel away some fifties and twenties and are utterly de-
jected to find no fives or tens smiling up at you.

Navigating Via del Comune proves unusually harrowing. Every time I return, I'm surprised anew at the steepness of this street, and as I begin my descent, my bag pulls up from behind me and goes skittering on ahead, almost yanking my arm from its socket. I have to wrestle it back under control and continue the journey as though I've got a lion on a leash. I've lately learned that the brucaioli actually do hold a dinner out here—each year on the night before the extraction of the three additional contrade to run the Palio. I can't imagine how they manage it. The tables must be set up on meticulously calibrated stilts. I'd like to see it, someday; though it will certainly be a dinner for which I do *not* volunteer for table service.

The Società's doors are open, and the lights are on. There's a coatrack, so I can finally stow my bag, and once I'm free of it I feel loose and limber and ready to rumble, like a boxer just entering the ring. It's still a bit early to expect Dario to be here, but I don't feel I need him. I can talk to anybody. I don't promise they'll entirely understand me, but I'm up to it.

It's the first time I've been here in autumn; it hadn't occurred to me that the chill night air might not be optimal for dining al fresco. And in fact the garden is empty. But I find rows of tables set up inside, in a large room I've never noticed before, across from the entry to the museum. A lot of women and teenagers are striding purposefully around its perimeter, laying place settings and unfolding chairs, and I feel a momentary impulse to offer my help; but then I see Silvia overseeing the preparations, and the recollection of how I performed the last time she engaged my services steals all my resolve. Instead, I decide to look for a bar.

The place is filling up now, lots of people coming in and

being hailed by friends and colleagues; bear hugs, double kisses . . . you'd think they hadn't seen each other in months, though they were probably all here just a few days ago. It's wonderful to see, but once again forbidding to encounter from the outside. Coats are shirked, circles are formed; the women seek out tables or sofas where they can sit and confer while the menfolk all make their way around the corner, where there's a TV and . . . a bar! It's pretty thick in here— thick and loud—but I insert myself into the mix anyway and make my way to the counter, where I hope to buy a little popularity by ordering up a round for myself and whoever might be so fortunate as to be at either elbow. I catch the bartender's eye—and I can see the momentary flicker of *who the hell is that?* before he starts making his way over . . . .

. . . And that's when I get out my wallet. And remember that there's nothing much left in it.

So I melt back into the crowd, slide my way past the various backs and buttocks, grab my coat, and head back outside to find an ATM. As I ascend Via del Comune, I pass little knots of people on their way in to the dinner. I recognize some of their faces, and it's clear that one or two recognize mine—or think they do; but they must then convince themselves they're wrong, because what would a Palio whore like me be doing here in November, and besides I'm going the wrong way. (The Sienese actually have a term for those who turn up only at Palio time: *tregiornisti,* or three-days.)

By the time I return, the dining room has begun to fill up. There's no sign yet of Dario, and I become aware that I'm faced with the unenviable prospect of finding someone to sit with. I'd hoped to grease my way into a party at the bar, but returning there now I find everyone tossing back their last mouthfuls. As I approach the counter I see, at last, a familiar face—that of Dario's friend Luigi, who sees me and furrows his brow. "You're a bit of a lurker, aren't you?" he says.

"How do you mean?"

"Furtive," he says. "You're here, then you're not here, then you're here again." He makes an embarrassing little creeping gesture with his hands curled under his chin. Obviously he saw me come in, doff my coat, and enter the bar; then come in again, doff my coat again, enter the bar again. Admittedly odd behavior, especially for someone who's basically an uninvited guest. I decide not even to attempt an explanation; nothing at all would be gained by it. Instead we make small talk for a few minutes—he asks how things are in America, as Italians often do, and I feel a momentary twinge of guilt that I can only really answer for my little corner of it; I've got to start paying more attention to what's going on in, say, Appalachia, or the Pacific Northwest.

Then he finishes his drink and leaves the bar—but does *not* go to the dining room, so I can't follow him to his table and plonk myself down with him and his friends, which had been my diabolical plan. Instead I'm left on my own, looking at the rows of tables, all of whose chairs seem happily filled, and the metaphor of being an outsider seems suddenly, appallingly concrete. I'm just thinking that maybe I'm not really hungry anyway and maybe, if I am, more tiny sandwiches on the Campo would do the trick, when who should appear, like an angel of mercy in a shiny white leather coat, but Luigina, impossibly stylish as ever and still the only person in this city who will actually shout my name with pleasure.

We embrace and kiss and exchange a few pleasantries, and then she says to me, "You need a place to sit?" And she starts looking around for someone into whose care she might deliver me; but as her eyes scan the room I can see her tally up four or five other people she has yet to greet—and I realize she's the president's wife, she has better things to do than look after me. Plus, I'm a grown man, for God's sake. So I tell her thanks, I'm fine, and send her off to fulfill her duties as hostess.

This suffuses me with a warm feeling of maturity and self-sacrifice but leaves me with my original dilemma. The volunteer waitstaff is in circulation now, serving the antipasti course. It's now or never.

Is there a more formidable task than inserting yourself into a group of tightly knit strangers in a place you don't belong? Yes, as it happens: inserting yourself into a group of tightly knit strangers in a place where you don't belong *and* you're lucky if you understand thirty percent of what anyone says to you. I force myself to put this into perspective: "We live in an expanding universe, rapidly succumbing to thermodynamic entropy; in five billion years the sun will go nova and none of this will matter anymore." So I dive in.

After a quick and increasingly disheartening tour of the room I get lucky and spot an open seat right across the table from Giuliano Ghiselli, the writer and TV host I met a few months back. I'm not at all surprised to find a place opposite him, because that may be the most vulnerable spot in the room; Giuliano is a handsome, silver-haired fellow, outwardly congenial, always smiling; seeing him amble up the street, you'd never think to be on your guard. But even a brief acquaintance is enough to reveal that his intellect is fierce, and he has the eyes of a warrior—they glint with readiness for combat. Fortunately for me, I'm so ill equipped an opponent he'll almost have to view me as a kind of charity case—like an idiot cousin or a friendly dog.

I reintroduce myself, and he flatters me by remembering me—he's not the type who would pretend otherwise if he didn't—so I'm welcomed to the table and meet the other men flanking him, who are all very welcoming. I've found my place, I can relax for a moment; and even better, there's a heaping platter of tuna bruschette to be dealt with.

Dinner proceeds apace—the next courses are polenta with meat sauce, braised beef, and white beans dressed with olive oil; have I mentioned that they eat *very* well in the contrada?—and Giuliano holds forth in so engaging a manner that it's distressing not to have any idea what he's talking about. He's got everyone around him in stitches. Once I make the mistake of laughing along as though I'm in on the joke, and he directs an additional bit of commentary directly at me, so that I'm forced into a series of ridiculous feints—dropping my food on my thigh, fussing with my napkin, pretending my cellphone is ringing. The problem, I eventually discern, is that Giuliano, being among other things a linguist, incorporates wordplay and witticisms into his everyday patter, which for a nonnative listener can feel a lot like being at the very end of an especially lengthy crack-the-whip. I mean, I really *have* made strides in my Tuscan, but I'm not anywhere near the point where I can twig to double entendres. I'm reminded of the time I took my friend Paola, a native Genovese, to a performance at the Chicago Shakespeare Theater; the play was *Love's Labour's Lost,* which is pretty much three acts' worth of Elizabethan puns, making it a challenge even for native English speakers. But for Paola, it was like slogging through mud into a swarm of bees. Right here, right now, I feel her pain.

After a few mouthfuls of wine I'm feeling quite contented and am even having conversations with some of my neighbors—specifically a dapper, genial fiftysomething named Enrico, who seems amused by not knowing what to make of me. He can't figure out why I'm here, and when I say "This, exactly this," I can tell he thinks I mean the polenta; so I make a sweeping gesture to take in the entire room and accidentally thwack a passing *nonna* right in the tush.

Before I can make too many such gaffes, everyone's attention is called to the head table. It's time for this Dinner with the Captain to be turned over to the host. Gianni is the opposite of Giuliano: reserved, terse, taciturn. It suits him and suits his role in the contrada—the captain being essentially the head coach, the man responsible for the actual performance at the Palio and thus the steward of the jockeys, the guardian of the horses, the handler of the super-double-secret negotiations, and so on. He needn't dazzle or charm, but he'd better be formidable. And Gianni certainly is; I've yet to dare to speak a word to him.

Gianni makes a few brief opening remarks and then introduces the special guests: Trecciolino, aka Gigi Bruschelli, who won the August 2003 and July 2005 Palii, both times riding the beloved Berio; and Gingillo, aka Giuseppe Zedde, who won last August riding Elisir di Logudoro.

Suddenly the atmosphere turns electric, and I realize why a stray American visitor wandering the perimeter of the room doesn't raise even a scintilla of interest. Trecciolino and Gingillo are, by the standards of the contrada, megastars. I feel it myself; after all, I witnessed firsthand two of the three victories these men are responsible for, and now here they are, close enough to touch.

Dario arrives just in time for this portion of the evening, and he too is starry-eyed at the sight of the two great fantini. We make a place for him at the table, which is easily enough done because a lot of people have got up and moved to where they can get a better view of the guests of honor. And they're worth seeing; Gingillo is a lean, fine-boned, almost pre-Raphaelite presence, though clearly with sinews of iron; and Trecciolino is a dark, smoldering matinee-idol type with the body of a bantamweight boxer. Just sitting there, they've got the crowd riveted. The risen Christ Himself could descend in a pillar of light and start playing bongos in the garden, and not a head would turn.

Gianni looks quite happy that the focus is off him tonight, since with the two fantini here it isn't likely that anyone's going to be putting him under the spotlight. But before he turns the mic over to the stars, he cues up a video replay of the last three victories.

Now, I'm dead certain that everyone in this room was either present at these races or has seen them many times since on television, or both. In fact, it wouldn't surprise me if they all knew every move of every horse at every moment of each race. Yet when the footage comes up on the monitor, it's as though they're all seeing it for the first time. There's shouting, gasping, cheering—and, at the end, wild applause. The mark of an exceptionally good drama, I think, is that it fully engages you even when you know how it ends. In that sense, the Palio is, for the brucaioli—for *all* the Sienese—an utterly compelling civic narrative, a kind of creation myth that just keeps on unfolding. They write two new chapters every summer, in big, broad strokes, then spend the rest of the year annotating.

Which brings us to the question-and-answer session, during which the fantini are peppered by a wide range of questions, some of them staggeringly specific ("Okay, I want to ask about your second time around the pass of San Martino, which was after the Dragon's rider had fallen off and you had the chance to really close in on the Goose . . . ."), some of which are intended to raise a laugh ("Now that we've given you two wins, if you ride for us again will you give us a discount?"), and one or two of which are uncomfortably loaded ("Who would you say is more responsible for your victories, you or the captain?"). It's all amiably high-spirited, even when the contrada's resident dipsomaniac, nicknamed Caio Buio, stands up and begins a rambling account that's part conjecture, part anecdote, part personal memory. Eventually the crowd starts to heckle him, and Giuliano shouts past me, *"Soggetto! Soggetto!"*—"Get to the point!" Caio Buio gives up with a shrug and sits back down. Personally, I think his enthusiasm just got the better of him; faced with his idols, he merely sought, as so many do, to claim their notice. But what most interests me is that, in this atmosphere of utter egalitarianism, it isn't Caio Buio's presence that sparks foment; it isn't his audacity in putting himself forward; it's his momentary descent into stream of consciousness. Elsewhere in the world, someone like him might fall through the cracks of society, but here, he belongs. He has a place. And no one can ever take it away from him.

Certainly there *is* a hierarchy within the contrada, but it's almost invisible to my eyes, and it seems based on something other than education or profession. It's more a meritocracy of the spirit. Those who are most willing to make themselves available to the others—who smile the most, shake the most hands, circulate and converse—seem to wear the green, gold, and blue with the most authority. By now I've come to recognize several of them, including more than a few I haven't even met yet.

On the drive back to Dario's house I ask about Salvatore Ladu, more familiarly known as Cianchino, the jockey who won the 1996 Palio and ended the contrada's forty-one-year losing streak. If there's a superhero for the Caterpillar, he has to be it. Dario tells me that in fact he had his two sons baptized in the contrada but hasn't been seen much there since. He's too busy at his own establishment, a pub in the area called Bar Valli. I make a note to try and get there for a drink.

Meantime, Dario tells me I'm in luck: there's another event in Società tomorrow, and another the night after that. I'm delighted to hear this, though a little surprised. "I thought the official contrada year was over," I say.

He looks at me oddly. "Well . . . yes," he says, as if having to explain this to a backward child. "But immediately after the contrada year ends, the new contrada year begins. There will be plenty of things going on: parties, dinners, celebrations . . . ." And he starts rattling them off, like a litany of glee. "There's the cena of the *sonetti,* the *cena degli auguri,* the *cena di Carnevale,* the *cena della stalla* that's held at the stables . . . ."

This is when jet lag finally claims me. I drift into a kind of semiconsciousness in which the headlamps of the oncoming cars become party lights and the sound of distant laughter rings in my ears. By the time we arrive, I feel as though I've not only heard about those celebrations but lived through them all, one right after another.

MAKE JUBILATION

. . .

I SPEND MOST OF THE NEXT DAY ACCOMPANYING DARIO on his various rounds. It's a busy time for his olive oil business (called Rasna after the ancient Etruscans), as this year's pressing is now ready to ship. New oil is a highly sought commodity—you see signs for it everywhere; *olio nuovo*—and with very good reason: it's absolutely freaking out-of-this-world delicious. The texture and weight are essentially the same as what we're used to in the United States, but the flavor is much stronger and more complex, both fruitier and pepperier. As with the best wine, the oil alters with exposure to the air, so the same bottle will taste slightly different at the end of the meal than it did at the beginning. November isn't traditionally a big month for tourism in Italy, but believe me, if people knew about *olio nuovo,* they'd be tripping over each other to get here.

Those who are in the know but can't make the trip pay a premium to order the oil right after it's pressed, and Dario is engaged in an ongoing, frenetic cycle of bottling, labeling, invoicing, and shipping. I lend a hand to the extent I'm able, but since I'm coming into the process late, the time it takes him to instruct me in anything is almost better spent doing it himself.

At the end of the day he's pretty thoroughly wiped out, so to relax he cracks open a bottle of Sangiovese and pops in a DVD of the 2003 victory celebrations. Earlier in the day I'd mentioned to him how seeing the race replayed at dinner last night had recalled the parade we'd happened to catch a few days later.

"Which parade?" he'd asked.

"The one around the Campo," I said. "After the victory."

"I know, but—what was the theme?"

"Music," I'd reminded him, amazed he could forget such a thing. "Because Berio the horse shares his name with Berio the composer. Remember? You were dressed as a penguin. And playing a flute. I also seem to recall a lack of pants."

"Oh, yes," he said. *"That* one."

I blinked. "Was there any other?"

"Oh, Rob," he'd said with a laugh; "don't you know the contrada by now?" In fact, I learned, there were more than half a dozen parades in the Piazza del Campo, each with a specific theme and held on consecutive days. And of course, in true Caterpillar style, they're all minutely documented—as I discover now, with the DVD unfolding before me.

The first parade took place the morning after the race. The jubilant brucaioli marched to drums and flutes and visited all the other contrade in triumph. "All of them?" I ask. "Even the Giraffe?"

"Technically we are no longer rivals," he says, "so yes, we visit the Giraffe." Then he adds, with a wry glint in his eye, "But we went there very early, before anyone was up." I laugh, and he says, "But in fact we don't visit all the contrade. We omit the Dragon and the Goose."

"Why?"

"We have no relationship with either of them. And the Goose actually discourages it. They don't march themselves when they win; and they don't want any other victors to come to them."

I purse my lips. "Friendly bunch."

"They're quite odd in a number of ways. For instance, their feud with the Tower is the only rivalry not between neighboring contrade; they don't share a border. Also, in every other contrada, women can—and do—hold high offices. In the Goose, they can't even vote. In fact, some the women of the Goose have stopped going to assemblies in protest."

"Wow. That's . . . what's the word? Reactionary?"

"They're not just the only governing body in Siena to exclude women; they're the only governing body in all of Europe." He shrugs. "It doesn't seem to faze them. Even when people call them the *contrada infamona*."

By now my attention is caught by the on-screen goings-on; the scene has changed to a new parade circling the Campo that has an unmistakably Yuletide theme. "Whoa," I say, "did we just jump forward a couple months?"

"No; this is the parade of August twentieth."

A posse of fur-draped carolers saunters by the camera. "But," I sputter in protest, "Siena in August is, like, a hundred degrees in the shade. Why would they choose a Christmas theme?"

"It was to taunt the other contrade. The message is '*We* won the Palio, but *you* don't have anything to celebrate till December.' " All I can say is, if what I see before me is a taunt, it's got to be one of the more elaborately orchestrated in human history. The revelers are costumed as Santa Claus (known here as Babbo Natale), elves, and angels; two women are dressed as the Virgin Mary, one of them visibly pregnant, and hold up signs reading MARIA PRIMA and MARIA DOPO ("Mary before" and "Mary after"). There are floats both large and small: gingerbread houses, gift-wrapped packages, igloos from the North Pole, you name it. And of course there's music throughout, holiday carols as well as the familiar contrada themes.

The scene now switches to the "musical maestro" parade, which is the one Jeffrey and I caught. Once again I get to witness Dario's waddling performance *senza pantaloni*. ("Why exactly *were* you pantsless?" I ask. His reply: "They wouldn't stay on.") As impressed as I was the first time around, I'm more so this time, for one significant reason. "This was the *day after* the Christmas-themed march?"

He nods as he swirls the wine in his glass. "Each night there was a dinner, where we would decide on the next day's theme. And then we would get to work."

Several hundred people deciding on a theme and then implementing it in one night—*after* dinner? This seems like a logistical impossibility to me. "Who coordinates that?"

"The Committee of Joy," he says; Silvia's people. If anyone could pull off a superhuman stunt like a new parade every day, it's her. And speaking of which, here comes the next in the chronology . . . .

"Elegant dress," Dario says. "We all wore our best attire." There are women in gowns, men in dinner jackets. A jazz band plays. Everyone looks sensational. I look for, and don't find, Luigina; but I can just imagine.

Another scene change. "The fifth day," Dario says.

" 'How We Used to Be.' Everyone dressed as they would in 1955, which was our last win before 1996." This intrigues me, because a majority of the marchers can't have been born till long after the fifties; but everyone gets into the spirit of the thing, with poodle skirts and leather jackets and flower-print housedresses and hats. Some of them carry giant deckle-edged frames around their torsos, as though they're Polaroid snapshots. Once again, music resonates everywhere, including a large dollop of midcentury hits. It's slightly surreal but completely enchanting.

"Sixth day," Dario narrates as the next segment commences, " 'All the World Is Yellow, Green, and Blue.' " In other words, international costumes in Caterpillar colors: Dutch girls with windmills, bullfighters with bulls, Eskimos with igloos, a Chinese dragon . . . it's all here, and it's all in the Bruco hues. Spectacular.

The seventh day's theme is technically "The Caterpillar Through the Centuries," but by now the standards seem to have relaxed, allowing for some fairly shaggy interpretations. I mean, there's an Egyptian mummy—predating the contrada's origin by a millennium or two—and some Flintstones characters as well, which either refers to prehistory (exacerbating the Egyptian problem) or the cartoons of the past few decades. The appearance of several members of the Simpsons seems to argue for the latter, but then I have to wonder what they were doing there at all; though with that hair, Marge Simpson could almost pass as a yellow, blue, and green caterpillar.

Anyway, it's all merry chaos and it looks like a hell of a lot of fun; I'd love to have been there. It seems impossible that anything can top this, so I'm betting this is the last parade, which Dario confirms it was—except for the *official* victory parade.

"That took place two months later. It started at the Fortezza and wound all through the city. We decided on a medieval theme. Each member had a specific role to portray; I was from the popolo and had to lead a sheep on a leash through the streets. The men even grew beards to get into character. That night we had a street party open to everyone, for which we produced medieval coins that our guests had to use after entering our territory. Every corner of the contrada was set up with expensive tableaux, period music, animals, and so on.

"That was the official victory parade. The official victory *dinner* took place the following day in Piazza San Francesco. The horse had a place of honor next to *il tavolo della signoria.* As is the custom, during the meal delegations arrived from our allied contrade—the Porcupine, the Tower, the Shell— bearing lavish gifts, such as wild boar and a precious sculpture, but they didn't dine with us. At the end of the dinner and after the speeches, there were fireworks.

"Then, some weeks after the victory dinner, we have the *cena dell'asta,* in which the pole that held the drappellone is ceremoniously presented to the captain; it's all he gets from the victory he so tirelessly worked to realize. And the *cena del piatto,* when we return to the town council the silver plate that was fixed above the drappellone. Then there's the backwards dinner, where we all cross-dress . . . ."

"This is going to go on a while, isn't it?" I ask, feeling my head start to throb.

He chuckles. "It would if I could remember all of them. A

Palio victory can easily prompt between seventy and eighty celebratory meals. And I'm certain there are people who take part in every one of them."

"It's amazing you're not all obese."

"Oh, everyone works far too hard for that. The amount of organization involved—you can imagine. Look, here." He shuttles forward to some new scenes of the interior of the San Francesco parking garage, where a dinner of some fifty brucaioli is taking place on one of the escalator landings.

"We decided that since the garage is in our territory, we should claim it," he explains. "So we moved in the tables, chairs, and food, then set up, served, and afterward cleaned up as though they were never there. It looks like everyone is enjoying himself, but believe me, there's a furious amount of effort that takes place behind the scenes." And in fact it does look like a fairly boisterous affair, with each passerby on his or her way up the escalators offered a glass of wine, and a guitarist (Claudio, the contrada's pied piper) leading the others in a recital of the contrada's greatest hits. At this point I'm wondering if it would even be possible for the Caterpillar to assemble without bursting into song.

At the start of the viewing Dario was dead tired from his labors, but now he's reenergized; he looks through his stack for another DVD. He finds one that features an outing undertaken by several members of the contrada, in fulfillment of a vow. They swore that if Berio gave the Caterpillar a victory, they'd travel twenty miles on foot to visit him at his stables. And here they are, making good. Of course they've got a cameraman along; in addition to being tireless songsters, the brucaioli are relentless self-chroniclers.

It's strange to see Gianni and the others trussed out in hiking gear; Sienese men—for that matter, Italian men—generally do not wear shorts. But a twenty-mile walk can be construed as an athletic undertaking, so I suppose it makes sense. Still, it seems odd to be confronted with so many of their knees.

Notwithstanding, it seems like a pretty happy fellowship, though I have to wonder how long the trek actually took them; their pace seems to be roughly that of a Roman emperor on progress, with the entire imperial court in train. They might've been on the road anywhere between five hours and a year and a half. Of course, when they reach the stables, there's a celebratory lunch. And much, much cosseting and adulation of Berio. PETA should see them now. Racing is, of course, a dangerous sport; but what else are these animals to do? They're racehorses; they need to *race*. We've bred them over the centuries for this specific endeavor; it's in their DNA. To argue that they mustn't race because of the risk involved is specious unless you also furnish a means by which they can find fulfillment—can achieve release for the imperative we've instilled in them.

I find myself actually speaking this aloud; a sign that the wine is beginning to take serious hold. Never mind, there's only Dario to hear, and in his case it's very much a matter of preaching to the choir. He's found something else for me now, a set of photographs of a recent Caterpillar pilgrimage to the Vatican, where the members enjoyed a special audience with the pope. One shot shows the blessing of one of the contrada's artifacts, an altarpiece adorned with the Madonna and child, with Benedict XVI flanked by both Fabio the rector and Gianni the captain. Dario points out, with a wry grin, that Gianni is wearing blue jeans.

I actually knew about this Roman jaunt; several of the brucaioli posted about it on Facebook—as they also regularly post about their parties, competitions, dinners, and expeditions. It all comes at me now, in a rush: the sheer dynamism and social energy of these people. How can I expect, dropping in on them every couple of months, to understand a thing about them—to comprehend for even a moment the kind of encompassing sense of community that drives its members not only through each day but through their entire lives? The prospect is not only daunting; it may be unobtainable.

I may be saying this aloud as well. But Dario isn't listening; he's wrapped up in his frustration at not finding something he's looking for. "There's another event," he says, filing through the plastic cases. "They bring the prize banner to the cemetery and present it to those who are no longer with us. Even in death, you remain part of the community. Ah!" He pulls a DVD from the pile and shows it to me. It's of the August 2003 race. "We've seen the celebrations," he says; "now let's see what it was all about."

"We just saw it last night," I remind him.

He gives me a look that says, *But not yet today,* and pops it into the player.

Watching it again—seeing the preliminaries unfold, the excitement, the phenomenon of an entire city holding its breath; the uncanny explosion of the race itself, with its cometlike velocity; the tsunamis of euphoria that sweep over the piazza afterward—we're utterly silent until Dario says, "What is it about the Palio that makes it so emotional? I'd feel this way even if I were watching the Giraffe win."

I completely understand him. The reason I've said nothing

is the lump in my throat; I'm overcome with a kind of ecstasy by transference. What I'm feeling is a vacation from my own problematic Americanness. I'm tapping into something that's utterly free of irony, of cynicism, of condescension. I'm allowing myself—*freeing* myself—to *believe*. There's a risk in giving yourself over, heart and mind, to something so new, but it's new only to me. To the Sienese, it's ancient. And if I needed a reason to trust my instincts, I could find it beaming from every one of their faces.

At last Dario's energy finally rushes out of him. He switches to the news and collapses in a heap. I seize this moment to drag myself up to my room and tumble into bed.

Lying there, with the light of the moon spilling over me like milk and the ceiling spinning so determinedly I can still see it after I shut my eyes, I wonder about this compulsion to connect—this urge to understand. Where does it come from? If it's from some deeper need in me, maybe I shouldn't look to the brucaioli to fulfill it—not immediately, anyway. Maybe it's up to me to make some gesture first, offer some sign of commitment, some pledge.

And that's when I remember my own victory vow from a year ago: I promised to walk from Vagliagli to Siena.

*H*ISTORY and *LEGEND*

· · ·

⚏ HAVING RENEWED MY ACQUAINTANCE WITH GIULIANO Ghiselli at the captain's dinner, it seems almost natural that he should show up the next morning on C3 Toscana, Siena's TV station, talking at me while I have my cup of orzo and biscuit as breezily as he addressed me the night of the *cena*. This, it turns out, is one of his documentaries—*Fra Cronaca e Leggenda,* or "Between History and Legend," in which he tours some of the less renowned streets and byways of Siena, offering conflicting accounts of how they've come to acquire their names, including both the official version and the folkloric alternative—most of which, Dario tells me, he just made up. He's an amiable, engaging host, and I enjoy myself tremendously, though the folkloric accounts all seem to hinge on idiomatic phrases that I don't really understand. But even through the thicket of wordplay it's clear that Giuliano knows Siena backward, forward, inside out, and upside down (and some of the camera angles make this quite explicit, to the point that I actually get a little dizzy).

So I arrange to meet him for a drink. He's a fount of knowledge on Caterpillar history and legend, and I'm eager to soak some of it up.

We're to rendezvous at the nameless bar the brucaioli patronize so loyally. Despite the briskness of the air I seat myself at one of the two small outdoor tables; it's still a kick for me, feeling sufficiently confident to place myself here at the literal crossroads of Caterpillar society, where you can see, and be seen by, everybody. Not that anybody much is out and about today; the streets are noticeably quieter in late autumn than they are in high summer. But that just makes it easier to spot Giuliano when he comes ambling up the street, hands folded behind him. After we greet each other and sit down, he initiates the first of many steps involved in lighting his pipe, a process which, for me, compares with the Japanese tea ceremony as an example of mere consumption elevated to civilized ritual. It takes a certain kind of man to smoke a pipe, a certain gravitas, which Giuliano, despite the nimbleness of his wit and his readiness to laugh, seems to possess in spades.

We get a round of drinks; I order a Sangiovese, thinking I still have to learn to drink like an Italian, but Giuliano pulls a fast one on me by ordering coffee. Too late for me to switch; but the Sangiovese will at least take the chill off. Then we get down to talking. I have a few very particular things to ask him, the first of which concerns the *Palio straordinario* of 1945, held in celebration of the end of World War II and hence called the *Palio di pace*—the Peace Palio. Ironically, it ended in a piazzawide fistfight—with the Caterpillar at the center of it. I of course understand that after so many years without a race (the contrada associations had essentially shut their doors at the outbreak of hostilities in 1939) there might be some long-suppressed tensions bubbling beneath the surface. But how did a Palio devoted to peace degenerate into the exact opposite?

"We were meant to win that Palio," says Giuliano. "The most coveted horses in the extraction were Folco and Mughetto; we got Mughetto, the Dragon got Folco. So we knew that they would be our principal rival. But the Dragon had won just four days earlier, in the Palio of August 16, whereas we hadn't won since 1922. So we felt that our time had come.

"Accordingly, we offered deals to all the other contrade to get them to support our victory. Only the Dragon and the Tortoise refused outright. Then, on the day of the race, the Tortoise took objection to a false start and withdrew from the race in protest. That left only the Dragon as a threat to our victory. Remember, they had won just four days earlier. They had no hunger for victory, not like we did. Our jockey, Biondo, offered theirs, Rubacuori, a huge sum of money—and this was in a time of postwar poverty, when such funds were scarce.

"Despite this, when the race began the Dragon immediately took the lead, followed by the Caterpillar, and thus it stayed all the way to the finish. At which point we exploded in anger. We chased Rubacuori around the piazza. Then we went and took the banner from the Dragon and shredded it. Perhaps inevitably, a brawl followed, which was so intense that even some of the soldiers of the Allied troops got involved.

"As a result, not only was the Caterpillar disqualified, but we were made to pay for a new drappellone, repainted by the original artist. But the scoundrel, when he depicted the Dragon on the banner, he put a tiny caterpillar on its tongue, can you imagine?"

That does seem more than usually provocative, even by

Sienese standards. "But the Caterpillar and the Dragon," I say, "you're not rivals today, as I understand it."

He waves a hand in dismissal. "There is no relationship," he declares. "None." So instead of the fire of animosity, there is the cold chill of mutual shunning. I'm not sure which is worse.

Giuliano has warmed to his topic and is smoking energetically; his eyes spark and flash, and inevitably he's speaking faster. It's become difficult for me to keep up. Part of me would like to follow this thread; I'm still not entirely certain how a contrada—any contrada—can feel righteous indignation with regard to another that has refused to let it fix a race. This is completely alien to every American notion of sportsmanship; but it is deeply, profoundly Sienese. It makes me feel as though I'll never truly belong here; that I've gone through a black hole to some alternate universe where the laws of physics are entirely different—where rain falls upward and people walk on their hands.

Rather than reveal my unworthiness to Giuliano, I decide to change the subject. Possibly I might ease him back into more measured cadences by asking about something farther back in history—specifically, the Bruco's official appellation: the Noble Contrada of the Caterpillar. Only three other contrade share this honorific (Eagle, Shell, and Goose, though a few others have earned titles other than "Noble"), and I was wondering what the Caterpillar had done to be so deserving. I've asked Dario, who explained that the title was awarded partly to reflect the brucaioli's valor in a Sienese victory over Florence in 1381 but that it also referred to some other signal event—"Ask Ghiselli," he encouraged me.

"It dates from the fourteenth century," Giuliano now says with confidence, "when Siena was ruled by the Council of Twelve. After a plague had nearly wiped out the population, the lives of the working class degenerated while the middle class thrived. This was particularly evident in the Caterpillar, which was part of the city's vital wool trade; the brucaioli were the principal wool carders. The ghettos in which we lived were so poor, and the government so unresponsive to our plight, that when they attempted to impose a new wool tax in 1371, it provoked a rebellion. We had simply been pushed too far. Barbicone, one of our civic heroes, organized a march on the *centro,* where we took control of the offices of government and even threw a city official from the top of the bell tower." He puffs contentedly on his pipe for a few moments, as though pausing to savor the spectacular ferocity of this particular punishment. "A new government was formed, representing all the social classes, and the Caterpillar was able to negotiate with this new coalition the construction of proper housing on our main street—which is why we call it Via del Comune. There's a statue of Barbicone in the grotto," he adds, nodding toward the fountain; so at last I've learned the identity of the heroic figure who stands beside the rampant caterpillar, wielding a sword as though directing traffic through eternity.

I find it very appealing that Giuliano speaks about the remote past with the same immediacy he does the near present. He's as engaged, emotionally, in the story of Barbicone as he is in the Peace Palio—the latter of which he gives the impression of having seen, though he would've had to be not much more than an infant. This is the kind of thing that makes these people so attractive to me; their history isn't something they've left behind them, it's part of an ongoing narrative in which they themselves are playing a vital part.

I ask Giuliano about the Caterpillar's lucky number. Every contrada has one, ranging from single digits (5 for Porcupine) up to 90 (Ram). The Caterpillar's is 45, and you find it everywhere in the contrada, spoken or inscribed like a totem or a prayer. My own theory is that it comes from the steep grade of Via del Comune, which can feel like forty-five degrees after a rollicking contrada dinner.

Apparently I've overestimated my ability to understand, because Giuliano starts explaining how the number is actually connected to Hebrew numerology—at least I think that's what he's saying—but my grasp of his meaning is irreparably shattered when Dario shows up and takes a seat. This is the way things go in the contrada: you sit, you drink, you talk, and someone inevitably comes and joins you. Street life— urbanity at its most appealing. Of course I'm Dario's houseguest, and hence he's my ride home, but I prefer for the moment to pretend that this is an entirely random encounter.

Dario seems a little surprised to find us immersed in a subject so arcane, and I realize it is a bit silly—I'm supposedly here to learn about the life of the contrada and assimilate into it, not write a doctoral thesis on Caterpillar symbols and iconography. Dario accordingly changes the subject to Beppe di Bedo, the legendary brucaiolo who collected Rose Rosa at the 1996 extraction and who by many accounts was the corporealization of the contrada's spirit: masculine, indomitable, immovable.

Giuliano smiles and refills his pipe, a sign that he's content to stay a while longer (I was worried I might be boring him).

"Now, *there* was a man," he says, smiling, and his eyes flash again. "I once caught him in a fistfight with someone twice his size. It was over a woman, of course. Beppe was a whirlwind; the other man couldn't seem to lay a hand on him. In fifteen minutes it was over, he'd beaten his opponent into the ground.

"He lacked the ability to feel pain," he adds, enjoying the memory. "He easily absorbed blows that would have killed any one of us. But then he was solid muscle, a real gladiator; punching him was like punching a brick wall."

The seductive tug of reminiscence eventually brings forth Giuliano's own personal history. "From 1956 through 1965, I was always one of the alfieri," he says. "You should have seen me back then; I was very lean and handsome." I believe it; he has the manner of someone who grew up confident in his good looks. "I was three times the *duce,* and once the *palafreniere,*" this being the man who accompanies the horse during the historical procession prior to the race, "despite my having no great affinity for horses. Also, if the occasion allowed, I was the drummer for the *giro della città,*" the tour of the city following a victory. "And I was often the page for Caterpillar weddings and funerals."

I can almost see him now—young, lithe, limber, at the head of an entire procession of brucaioli, marching right past where we're seated now—these very walls reverberating with his steady rat-a-tat-tat, these cobblestones clattering with the footfalls of dozens—no, hundreds—of contradaioli: men, women, children; entire families, old men doddering on canes, children racing ahead of their parents, breathless and exhilarated. It's a scene that recurs here so often, perhaps the fabric of the time has become saturated; perhaps I really am seeing the past bleed through to the present. Beppe di Bedo, with arms like steel cables and a small coterie of adoring women in his wake . . . Barbicone, his head held high in triumph, carrying on his shoulder a child whose future is immeasurably brighter because of him . . . the brawlers of the Peace Palio, missing teeth and flecked with blood, waving aloft the tatters of the contested banner . . . .

Maybe that's why the brucaioli frequent this little *sala da tè,* after all. So much volatility, so much volubility, so much of the raw stuff of *life* has filed past this humble stoop on its way into myth and legend. This is the place to hear its echoes— and to enjoy a front-row seat for the next round, when the time comes.

MUSEUM PEACE

. . .

⚌ I FIND MYSELF BACK IN SOCIETÀ L'ALBA THE NEXT NIGHT for an assembly. These are held regularly to discuss contrada business, and by a stroke of luck this month's coincides with my visit here. I arrive with Dario, who does not as a rule attend these events but who kindly agrees to stay and steer me through this one.

Apparently he's not the only brucaiolo to take a pass on these things, because the room isn't quite half filled. Fabio and Gianni are here, of course, as are Giorgio and some of the other officials, and of course Luigina, who greets me with slightly less ebulliance than usual. I take that as a good thing; it means she no longer finds it quite so remarkable a thing to see me.

Silvia takes over the meeting early, and I discover to my dismay that it's primarily fiscal in nature; the only thing more stupefyingly dull than financial accounts are financial accounts being given in a language you only partially understand.

Yet this is no everyday operations budget under discussion. It's rather an account of the funds paid out for the last Bao Bello, which, Dario whispers to me, is an extravagant party the contrada throws every year in its gardens, to which anyone and everyone is invited. (*Baco,* or *bao* for short, means "worm"; this is what the Giraffe used to call the Caterpillar when they were enemies. In the time-honored way of truly spirited people, the brucaioli embraced the term used against them and named their annual feast "Beautiful Worm.")

I'm not sure what he means by "extravagant party" until I see the expenses projected on-screen. There are healthy sums attached to such line items as American Bar, Aperitif Bar, Osteria, Pizzeria, Ristorante, Barbecue Bar, Pub, Barberi (a kind of ball game), and Ice Cream Stand—at which point I lose track.

But it appears there's plenty to discuss tonight. Some of those in attendance—a couple of younger guys in particular— are very vocal about the way the Bao Bello has degenerated into a kind of free-for-all. People arrive already drunk, and when the Caterpillars in attendance try to quell any nascent troubles, they're disrespected—sometimes to the point of threats—right here on their own home turf. I can't entirely follow the back-and-forth of the discussion, which flies like a volleyball between the complainants on one side and Fabio and Silvia on the other; but I can understand the nature of the grievances. I can also understand the frustration of the officials, who ask, quite reasonably, What do you suggest? Should we cancel Bao Bello entirely because of these troublemakers? That seems the only conceivable solution. It can't become an invitational, with guests presenting their tickets at the door; that would undermine the whole spirit of the event.

The discussion achieves even more velocity, so that soon I'm hearing nothing more than a rapid volley of vowel sounds. I choose the moment to slip out to the lavatory. On my way back to the meeting room, I pause and look around me: the place is so empty—so still. I've never had the chance to see it this way before. I decide to take a quick tour of the museum, which occupies the levels above me. The last time I was here, some fifteen months ago, the place was packed with revelers celebrating the Caterpillar victory. Now there's no one.

In this exhilarating absence I can see, for the first time, the graceful outlines of the interior. These are the work of the architect Lorenzo Borgogni, who in 1967 hollowed out this ancient edifice—it was built in 1670—and in its place erected the swooping arches and columns of the first Bruco museum. It retains the rough, masculine character of the city and its people—it's all done in the ubiquitous red brick you see everywhere here—but it has a lightness and grace you can only call athletic, fitting for a people so devoted to sport and to the muscular sensuality of horseflesh in particular.

In the early twenty-first century, Borgogni's museum was thoroughly renovated and amplified, giving it a spare, minimalist makeover that's both completely modern and, I think, quite beautiful. The space is centered around a spiral staircase that seems suspended on nothing more than its own dazzling audacity; it looks like a scarf floating on a breeze. I climb it to the gallery that runs around the perimeter of the place, where the treasures, relics, and totems of past centuries are gathered behind sheets of glass, against backgrounds of translucent white. The contrast between the heavy, ornate, color-saturated artifacts and their new airy, almost weightless context provokes a wonderful frisson; it's as though the potent, powerful history on display here is contained by nothing more than a thought—which of course is very nearly the case. There's nothing here that would seem wildly out of

place in the life of the streets beyond. Gold crosses, silver reli-
quaries, coats of arms, devotional tablets, altarpieces, chalices,
chargers, censers, banners . . . and of course vestments, which
form the bulk of the collection and anchor it on each of the
three levels. Tunics, doublets, jackets, hose, caps and capes,
hats and helmets, shoes and boots; all of them vibrant and rich
with embroidery and detail. There are even suits of armor;
hell, there are kits for horses, including some saddles so splen-
did you'd think Versace had an equestrian line. And it's all
akin to what you'll still see in a modern Palio procession;
there are ensembles here for the barbaresco, the alfieri, the
pages, the duce, everyone. I've been to Mardi Gras in West
Hollywood, and let me tell you, those boys could *learn* something here.

There are artworks too: Giuseppe Nicola Nasini's *Saint
Bernard* and *Saint Catherine of Siena;* Luca di Tommè's *Madonna
and Child;* Dionisio Montorselli's spectacular *Adoration of the
Magi* and *Circumcision of Jesus;* but perhaps the canvas that
most arrests me is a relatively recent work, a 1967 triptych in
tempera by one E. Cesarini, *Barbicone and the Brucaioli in the
Uprising of 1371,* whose largest panel shows the Bruco hero
hurling a representative of the Council of Twelve out the
window of the Torre del Mangia—with the Campo spread
out below in almost literally dizzying contrast.

And suddenly I find myself among the drappelloni—the
raison d'être for this whole edifice and the centerpiece not
only of the collection but of the contrada's sense of self. This
long aisle of silken banners is the spine of the Caterpillar's lore
and legend, its one constant and irrefutable value; and again it
hits me with the force of a revelation that here is a people—
not just the brucaioli but all the contradaioli, all the Sienese—

whose history, while marked by war and disorder and occupation and civic strife, isn't defined by any of those things; it's defined by a competition. By a *game*. One that provides them a constant source of renewal and of hope. Is it any wonder they seem to be the happiest, most self-reliant people I've ever met?

The earliest banner I can find is August 1763. It's a little the worse for wear, part of its bottom third having rotted away. The succeeding drappelloni are in better condition: July 1792 . . . July 1814 . . . July 1816 . . . July 1826 . . . they all look fairly similar, as though there's a set pattern for the design: the Virgin Mary at the summit, suspended in clouds like Mary Poppins and crowned by stars; and three different coats of arms descending beneath her. At the very bottom, there's the date; and around the entirety of the banner, a decorative border. Slight variations occur over the hundred-odd years that follow, but it isn't till 1894 that there's a banner completely at variance with those before it. This one boasts an image of Saint Francis looming like Godzilla over the Basilica di San Francesco, which reopened that year after significant restoration work. It's notable, however, that this was a *Palio straordinario,* raced on August 19, three days after the traditional Palio of the Assumption, so maybe the design was allowed to be *straordinario* as well.

As I glide along the galleries, victories passing by me in mind-numbing profusion, I lose all track of time, until I'm roughly snapped back to the latter by the sudden dousing of the electrical power.

I realize the assembly must have ended and the attendees all gotten up and departed. Whoever's last out the door has simply flicked off the switch. I'm about thirty seconds from being locked in—and I know, from a steady diet of Hollywood movies, that no good can come of spending a night in a museum. Already, the costumes around me—so vital and present under halogens—seem, in their barely perceptible silhouettes, to be slightly moving.

I fumble my way along the galleries, guiding myself by the railing that is all that stands between me and a significant plummet to the ground floor. I have a rough sense of where I'm going, and when I reach the staircase I launch into a clattering descent that's just a hair too urgent—so that I miscalculate the curve of the structure, turn my ankle, and lurch forward. I'm falling down a flight of fairly unyielding steps, and it occurs to me that the impact will very likely dash the brains from my head—presuming I have any in there, which is beginning to seem arguable.

But as I flail away like a chicken with its wings clipped, I manage to grasp the banister and halt my fall before any damage is done. Having righted myself, I proceed more carefully, and when I reach the bottom of the staircase I grope my way toward the exit, through which the white light of the street beyond spills enticingly. I slow my step, calm my heartbeat, and try not to wince as I walk on my twisted ankle toward the door. I can hear the muted cadences of a conversation just beyond it, and when I arrive I see Dario in the street, having a cigar with a couple of other Caterpillars. I exit as casually as I can, and no one seems to think it at all unusual that I should be swanning out of their clubhouse after everyone else has headed home.

So there's an upside to not being noticed much; you don't register when you've just been an idiot.

DEUS EX MACHINA

. . .

⚒ HAVING STUFFED MY HEAD WITH THE ENTIRE CONTENTS of the Caterpillar museum, I feel a need to digest, mentally. I crave both a space of time and a geographical space that are essentially clear. So this morning I make the decision to walk. Dario has another full day of oil-related errands to run, and I've become aware that my coming along doesn't really do much to help him. And though he offers to drop me in Siena, there's nothing pressing for me to do there; the life of the contrada doesn't percolate on an autumn weekday the way it does on a summer holiday.

Which makes it the perfect day to make good my vow of last year. I will walk from Vagliagli to Siena, from Dario's front door to the door of the Società L'Alba in Via del Comune. I will appease the gods to whom I offered this act in exchange for a Caterpillar victory last August.

Did I say it was a perfect day for a walk? It isn't, entirely. There's a battleship gray cast to the sky that doesn't augur well, but the way the clouds are filtering the sunlight makes the rolling hills of Chianti seem more lushly, deeply green. Even at the worst of times—and I've seen it suffering from heat and drought, when it's been burned to brown straw—

it's a landscape that ravishes; but today it looks positively Edenic.

The only snag is that I don't really know how to get from A to B. I ask Dario to sketch out some directions for me, but he's wrapped up in trying to get himself out the door; he says instead, "It's very simple, you just go to Borgo Scopeto and take a right, and keep walking till you get to——" I'm so busy summoning up a visual of Borgo Scopeto that I miss the rest of the directions, and I don't want to hold him up by asking him to repeat them. And besides, there's a part of me that really doesn't mind just throwing myself out into the open air and riding where the wind will take me.

After Dario's gone I grab an apple and a bottle of water and put them in my backpack, along with an anorak from Old Navy, which cleverly folds into a little zippered pouch. Finally, I knot my fazzoletto around my neck and tuck it under my sweater, like an ascot. I figure it's suitable attire, since my trek is a debt of honor to the contrada. And then I set forth.

Borgo Scopeto is an expansive Tuscan vineyard and estate. Several years ago, when the American economy was booming, Jeffrey and I stayed at its hotel, the Relais Borgo Scopeto, along with two of my sisters and their husbands; they're all wine aficionados who the year before had invited us to join them in Napa, and we returned the favor by escorting them to *our* favorite wine country. The Borgo was so exquisite a location—like something from a Merchant-Ivory movie or a better-than-average season of *The Bachelor*—that for the first two days we didn't leave it. We even dined there (the restaurant is sensational).

Walking past the property now, I can't help marking the irony: the economy—not just America's, the world's—has taken a severe clobbering, and accordingly, rather than motoring up Borgo Scopeto's majestic drive in a rented Alfa Romeo, I'm hiking past it on foot, in my grubby jeans and dirty boots.

Yet I'm equally happy, possibly a bit more so. There's something about crossing a terrain under your own power that's like claiming ownership of it. The air is crisp, the breeze gentle; the sun, when it chances to spill through a temporary opening in the clouds, warm and buttery. There's a heaviness to the air that feels a bit threatening, but there's no telling when, or whether, it might give way to anything, so I choose to ignore it.

I pass through Pievasciata, a sleepy little community nestled in the hills and olive groves, and am accordingly enchanted. So much so that I end up missing a turn and walk about three miles out of my way before I realize it; trudging back is a little dispiriting (and in fact I introduce the Tuscan countryside to a whole spate of American expletives it's unlikely to have heard before), so I look for a place to sit and eat my apple. There are lots of picturesque nooks along the side of the road, outcroppings of rock beneath the shade of patchwork-colored trees; spots where songbirds might flutter down and sit happily on your finger, Disney movie style. But I'm looking for something not quite so Hallmark card— something a bit harder-edged. Someplace that reflects not only the splendor of the Chianti hills but the hardscrabble life those hills demand of those who work them.

I find such a spot some twenty minutes later: a gravel patch by the side of the road where somebody's ancient lorry has limped to die. Perhaps the owner is coming back to fetch its carcass, I don't know, but in the meantime, it calls to me. I prop myself on the flatbed, hook my heels on the rusted bumper, and dig my apple from my backpack as all around me the trees stir and hiss.

While I snack, I read a small, battered paperback I bought a few years back, an abbreviated history of Siena by Giuliano Catoni. The cover and title page have long since fallen off, but it's traveled with me every time I've come back here. I've probably read the entire thing several times by now, but never in order and not all at once; I just like to dip into a section or chapter and go from there.

This time I end up reading about Violante of Bavaria, a German princess who married the heir to the Tuscan throne in 1689 only to find herself both widowed and childless in 1713. She considered returning to her own country, especially when she heard that her sister-in-law, the Electress Anna Maria Luisa de' Medici (the name is a mouthful, the woman a handful), was returning to court and would have precedence over her. The two ladies weren't exactly gal pals, it seems.

But Violante's father-in-law, Grand Duke Cosimo III, persuaded her to stay and appointed her governor of Siena in 1717. And that's when she surprised everyone by displaying a genuine flair for administration. In fact, she became an instrumental figure in the history of the city, codifying the rites of the Palio and officially defining the number, names, and boundaries of the contrade—pronouncements that remain in effect to this day.

When Cosimo III died five years later, his son Gian Gastone succeeded to the throne. This new grand duke sent his bitchy sister, the electress, packing, and called his former sister-in-law Violante back to Florence. And since he preferred to spend most of his days in bed (as really, given the choice, who wouldn't?), Violante became his proxy and was at the center of a glittering court life, making her one of the most active and influential women in all of Europe.

How was Violante greeted by the people of Siena, I wonder. Did they accept her at once, or did she have to earn their respect? Did they grow to love her? Did they ever completely trust her? She was, after all, not Sienese—not even Italian—and was moreover a woman, put in a place of supreme authority over this most masculine of cities. As an American man, just trying in the humblest way possible to make a few friends among a small subgroup of this very proud and self-contained people and enjoying only incremental gains, I have to wonder what it was like for a Teutonic female to come riding up to the Palazzo Pubblico, drop all eight hundred and six trunks of her wardrobe, and then turn to the populace and say, "Hiya, I'm the new boss of you." Unless the Sienese have changed very much over the centuries (which I personally have to doubt), that must have gone over like the most leaden of lead balloons.

Speaking of lead balloons, that's what the clouds are now beginning to resemble. I've finished my apple, so I toss the core aside, return the book to the backpack and the backpack to my shoulders, and head out again. There's a low rumble in the distance, but not distant enough to reassure me, so I pick up my pace.

I'm still thinking about Siena in the eighteenth century when the first spatterings of rain snap me back to the present; then I stop under a tree to don my anorak. And that's when I look up and realize I've done it again; instead of retracing my steps to the path I shouldn't have left in the first place, I've made another wrong turn somewhere and am now hopelessly lost in the Chianti countryside. In a momentary panic, I pull out my phone to call Dario; but what's he supposed to do, come and get me? I don't even know where I am.

I decide to forge ahead—and why not? Turning back doesn't ever seem to work for me—and so I plunge into the open air as the rain increases in force, incrementally but noticeably.

Soon it's coming down in sheets—not so much cats and dogs as antelope and wolverines—and my anorak is clinging to me like a second skin. My body heat rises, and despite the coolness of the day I start perspiring. Sweat runs down my forehead, along the crook of my nose, and collects in my mustache. Before long I'm as drenched as if I weren't wearing the anorak at all. I come to a full stop and just stand there by the side of the road, the rain pounding on my head, my clothes sticking damply to my skin, my boots now twice as heavy for the load of mud they've accrued along the way. My ankle, which I twisted last night at the museum, begins to ache from the added weight.

Why am I doing this? It's not as though anyone is watching me, and even if someone were, it's unlikely they'd be impressed. I made a silly vow, and in my head it became something more than it ever should have. Who am I to make a promise in exchange for a Caterpillar victory? I'm not one of them. And to feel I have to honor my word? What presumption. As if the victory of August 2008 had hinged on me. As if I had anything even remotely to do with it.

I feel stupid and sad, standing in this downpour in the middle of nowhere, for no reason and to no conceivable gain.

I remain that way till the rain at last lets up a bit; then I continue slogging along, my spirit sapped, my will to live diminished by roughly half.

Some minutes later I see horses. Magnificent beasts, gleaming in the muted light, clomping about and whisking their tails and kicking up clots of newly wet earth. They're everything I'm not right now—carefree, weightless, belonging exactly where they are. It's irresistible. I stop to look at them and try to see them as the Sienese do—to gauge their strength and speed and stamina—but my eyes are too untrained. I see just beauty and grace and freedom.

I feel immeasurably better, maybe because I'm suddenly a bit light-headed. The horses move away from me so that I can't see them anymore, but I'm not ready to let go of them yet. So I turn up a gravel drive to follow them.

It's a very long drive, as it turns out, and I've gone a considerable way down its length without any more sight of the horses, so that I'm wondering if maybe I'd better just give up and turn around. And that's when someone speaks to me.

I turn and see a man a dozen or so yards away; he looks like a rancher—jeans, boots, hat. He repeats what he just said to me, but I still don't catch it.

"Sorry," I say, "I'm a little bit lost. I saw the horses." I point to where there quite plainly aren't any horses. "I got caught in the rain." I'm aware even as I say this that I'm sounding rather incoherent.

The rancher nods dubiously, and asks where I'm going.

"Siena," I say.

"Siena?" he repeats incredulously, and he glances past me as though he might spot a car he overlooked before.

I'm about to explain that I'm walking there for private

reasons and that I don't know the way and could use a bit of help with directions. But then he takes off his hat to wipe his brow, and I notice his face. It's very familiar. Dark eyes, square jaw . . . a kind of movie-star handsomeness . . . I know I've seen him before. And pretty recently, too.

Then it hits me. "Aren't you Trecciolino?" I ask.

He nods warily. "Yes."

"I just saw you a few days ago," I say, excited. "At Gianni Falciani's dinner, in the Bruco—with Gingillo."

He cocks his head. "You were there?"

"Yes; I'm an American, a friend of the contrada. I'm just visiting." I point back to the road. "In fact, I'm walking to Siena to fulfill a promise I made before the victory last year."

At least, that's what I think I'm saying. God knows what actually reaches his ears. He grins widely, as though listening to a parakeet try to speak Latin, but then he gestures toward the house and asks if I'd like to come inside and dry out a bit.

My first, intimidated impulse is to decline, because— because this is *Trecciolino,* this is Gigi Bruschelli, winner of eleven Palii and the jockey who gave the Caterpillar *two* of its last three victories, in 2003 and 2005, both with the same noble mount, Berio.

Yet how can I say no? Just thirty minutes ago I was moaning about how little anything I do, or say, or *feel,* matters in the grand arc of the Caterpillar narrative, and now here's Trecciolino, appearing virtually out of nowhere, a sudden benediction, a sign from above.

"Va bene, grazie," I say.

And with that he leads me up the walk to his house.

Now, one of the singular differences between Tuscany and the average American locality is that here the great majority of the social life occurs out in the open, in public spaces; or, in the case of Siena, in the great contrada halls. For that reason I haven't seen the interior of too many houses. Even so, the moment I step across Trecciolino's threshold, I know I'm seeing something extraordinary. It's large, airy, and open, with high ceilings and a suspended staircase and a dazzling array of equestrian memorabilia: sculptures, trophies, photographs, you name it. The furnishings are modern and sleek; what it most reminds me of is a classic California ranch house, circa the 1940s. I clumsily doff my mud-caked boots so that I don't defile the pristine blond wood floor, and peel off my anorak.

In the living room, a locomotive-length sofa winds around the perimeter of the room; behind it, there's a dining room table that could easily seat your average extended Italian clan—or a full marching band. And against the far wall is an anomaly: an enormous wooden wheel, which Trecciolino now tells me is seven hundred square meters across. "This place used to be a mill before I converted it," he explains. "There are still canals running underneath the place."

At this point his companion, Annarita, appears. She's as good-looking as he is; a svelte, olive-skinned beauty with a cascade of silken black hair. I'm more acutely aware than ever that I'm a moist, muddy, disheveled intruder who speaks in tangled phrases, but there's not even a hint of distaste or distrust in Annarita's eyes. Trecciolino explains me to her, and I become aware I haven't actually told him my name, so I do so now and shake the hands of both. Annarita leaves and reappears a few minutes later with a steaming espresso.

In the meantime Trecciolino shows me around the house, in particular the gallery of Palio photos that form a kind of Bayeux tapestry of his career in the Piazza del Campo. He's raced, and won, for a number of contrade, and each of his eleven victories is represented here, the blur of their colors immediately identifiable to us cognoscenti: the blue and yellow of the Tortoise; the burgundy, blue, and white of the Tower; the red, black, and blue of Porcupine; the orange, white, and azure of the Unicorn; the green, red, and white of the Goose; and, of course, the blue, green, and gold of the Caterpillar.

He seems justifiably proud of his victories—there are, after all, only two jockeys in Palio history who have racked up more (and since he's still racing, he could conceivably surpass them). Yet this is nothing to the pride that beams from his face when he tells me, "I was born and raised in Siena, you know. Not many who race the Palio can say that."

At one point a torrent of teenage boys roars down the staircase, and I suddenly realize that there's a rhythm to life here that I've been interrupting. I thank Trecciolino warmly for his hospitality—he responds with a dazzling smile, and his charisma is so overpowering that I miss one of the steps in the foyer and lurch forward, managing somehow to arrest my plummet just before slamming into the floor and breaking my nose. He coolly pretends not to have noticed.

Annarita comes to say goodbye as I'm pulling on my boots. Unfortunately, my anorak seems to have blown away (I'd left it on the stoop), though I'm less concerned about meeting further rain without it than about polluting Trecciolino's pristine acreage.

He walks me out to the drive, pointing out his stables and the living quarters where he has four apprentice jockeys in residence. As a final treat, I get to see his horses again; they appear out of nowhere, trotting up to the fence all brilliant and dark-eyed and quivering.

Trecciolino surprises me by offering to give me a lift to Siena, and as tempting as that may be, I have to decline. I've vowed to walk, and walk I must. Especially now that I've had this validation, this nod of approval from the Fates. I am on my own personal road to Damascus, and a vision has appeared, not to tell me to turn back but to give me courage to go forward.

Trecciolino smiles; he seems to appreciate my gumption and my devotion to the contrada. And so, armed with a few general directions from Gigi Bruschelli himself, I resume my walk.

The next hour or two pass pleasantly enough; there's a kind of electric tang in the air, as is often the case after a rainstorm, and it energizes me. But soon the terrain makes a drastic change. The winding, isolated country roads winnow away, and I find myself on a busy *strada statale,* which seems, after the bramble-covered paths I've just left, like the L.A. turnpike. I creep my way along a shoulder no wider than the average pants leg. Trucks come barreling by at something close to planetary escape velocity, and there's really nowhere for me to go—the best I can do is sort of lean out of their way. Even worse, by my estimation I'm only two-thirds of the way to Siena.

And this, of course, is when the sky decides to open and pour down upon my head a deluge of almost biblical proportions. It lasts only about five minutes, but that's more than enough to leave me thoroughly drenched. And there's no chance of drying out in the aftermath, because the tires of each truck that passes shoot a frigid sheet of water over me.

Many temporary heart cessations later, I reach the outskirts of the city, and my sense of arrival is somewhat dulled by my realization that I still have quite a few hilly miles to go before I reach the centro storico. At least the clouds have cleared, and the sun has come out. But it's still November, and the chill air reacts with the moisture in my clothes to produce a state of almost primal misery.

But when I reach the Porta Ovile, I feel a glow of triumph that transcends every hardship. It's taken me four hours and twenty minutes, I'm soaked through, I'm sweating, and my teeth are chattering, but I've done it; I've honored my vow, I've repaid the powers, divine or otherwise, who gave the Caterpillar its last victory. As I climb up the sharp incline of Via del Comune, I think how nice it would be if someone here knew what I'd just accomplished and offered a handshake for it; but then, that isn't the point. I haven't undertaken this for recognition or approval. I've done it solely for honor.

And of course I've had coffee at Trecciolino's house. I'd have to be crazy to ask for any further validation.

I'm very, very hungry now and feel I've earned a really good late lunch. I choose a restaurant called Medio Evo on Via dei Rossi. I must alarm the maître d'—I'm dirty and damp, with sweat running down my face—but he graciously doesn't show it.

A prosecco helps restore my equilibrium; a second one helps even more. And then there are stuffed onions, pappardelle with wild boar sauce, and a Chianti Classico to wash it all down. All under a vaulted ceiling with the crests of neighboring cities painted there: Arezzo, Montalcino, Pisa, Grosseto. I wonder what it would be like to walk to such places. Maybe if the Caterpillar were to win again next year. . . .

M Y   W A Y

. . .

I'M COMING TO THE END OF ANOTHER SOJOURN IN SIENA, but with no corresponding sense of completion. Despite the activity in Società L'Alba, I haven't made nearly as much headway as I'd hoped. On my way down Via dei Rossi, I spot a white plastic grocery bag skittering about a cul de sac, being blown first hither, then thither, then back again to repeat the circuit, always in frantic motion but never actually getting anywhere. "Brother, I know how you feel," I mutter as I pass; then after a few steps I turn back, pick it up, and stuff it into the first trash can I find. Maybe, by the rules of karma, someone will now do the same for me.

I'm attending one last event in the Società tonight: a dinner/karaoke contest. There are five teams competing, of which one comprises Luigina and me. She very kindly offered to be my duet partner, and if nothing else, singing with the wife of the society's president ought to put me on the map. But Luigina's offer isn't entirely an act of kindness; like all the Sienese, she's fiercely competitive, and she knows that back in America I have a second career as a singer. I front an alt-rock band called 7th Kind, which boasts three trumpets and two saxes. When you sing with that many horns, you learn pretty quickly how to make yourself heard. If I don't gain any immediate notice for singing with Luigina, I'll get it when I blow everyone's hair back from their heads.

When I arrive at the Società, I head to the bar, which is packed with men (women seem rarely to venture here). I make friends in the time-honored way—by buying a drink for whoever's on either side of me—and soon find myself drawn into a conversation with an older brucaiolo named Antonio. He has a brown paper sack that he's clutching jealously, and after we've chatted for a while he deems me sufficiently trustworthy to have a look at what he's got inside. It's a bottle of grappa, "my own home brew," he tells me proudly.

It's not every day you meet someone who brings his own hootch to a bar; I have to wonder what the point might be. But it turns out he's not drinking it here; instead, he slips it back into the bag to save for dinner. I get the distinct impression that the humble table wine the contrada serves doesn't pack enough punch for him. Meantime, he allows me to buy him another shot.

Once again I experience the phenomenon of my comprehension of the Tuscan dialect improving after a drink or two. Before long Antonio and I are holed up in a corner and he's showing me photos of his entire family, including his late wife. She has a lovely smile, and I tell him so.

Dario arrives, wearing a suit—he's just come from some business meeting or other—and this makes for so unusual a sight that he's subjected to a few minutes of collegial razzing. Then he announces that Rachel is on a bus from Rome and will be here within a matter of hours. You can actually feel the sudden welling up of joy; it's as though someone has released more oxygen into the room. I had no idea Rachel had become *that* popular. I feel something small and hard turn in my gut; a kind of presentiment—it's hard to say of what. But I feel as though I've just taken three wild swings and struck out, while the batter behind me has knocked it out of the park.

At dinner I take a seat close to Luigina so that we can confer on our performance, but I'm distracted by the first course—white-beans-and-bread soup, with a drizzling of olive oil—have I mentioned that they eat *very* well in the contrada?—and Luigina is distracted by being available to everyone, first-lady style. But it doesn't matter; after all, this isn't *American Idol*. It isn't American anything, as I find out, when we're called up to do our number. Luigina had requested that we sing "My Way," a tune for which she apparently has some fondness and which I know fairly well. But when Claudio starts up the recording and the lyrics appear on the screen, they're in Italian. I hadn't anticipated that. Suddenly I have to keep one step ahead, trying to figure out where to place syllables in the course of each measure, because the stresses aren't remotely the same as in the English original. For instance, the line

> For what is man / What has he got
> If not himself / Then he has not . . . .

becomes, in the Italian version:

> *A cose serve un uomo / Che cosa ha*
> *Se non se stesso / Allore lui non è niente* . . . .

I'm like a juggler who's suddenly been tossed a half-dozen extra balls. Also, the tune is in a spectacularly wrong key for me, pitching way too high on the climactic notes. But it suits Luigina fine; she croons along in a kind of husky Lauren Bacall purr.

Eventually I just give up the melody and humbly take the backseat, singing harmony; and what do you know, *that's* what gets everybody's attention. I thought, from all my years of watching the San Remo Festival, that the way to an Italian audience's heart was through bigness, crescendo; but right here and now, it's the subtlety of singing thirds and fifths that wins them over.

Of course, the song is designed for a supersize finish, and we make the most of it, after which there's exactly the kind of ovation I'd hoped for; finally, *finally* I've made the brucaioli sit up in their chairs and see me as something more than a tourist.

"I'm Sonny," I tell Luigina as I scoop her into an embrace, "and you're my Cher." Which even she thinks is funny, because she must be two heads shorter than the diva in question.

A few more teams perform, after which three finalists are called on to do another number. The first is a trio of three lissome young girls, who perform an Italian number I haven't heard before with a fair amount of jumping up and down. The second is another duo, the male half of which is the former captain, Riccardo Pagni—the man who ended the Bruco's dry spell with the victory of '96—and he's actually a threat; he has a smooth, easy voice and a very winning stage presence.

I can feel my pulse thrumming in my wrist, and my mouth has gone dry in anticipation. I'm pretty sure, by the reception to our number, that Luigina and I will be the third finalist team. But if we're not, I have to accept it, I have to laugh and applaud and show what a good sport I am.

Claudio announces the third team: "Luigina e Robert." Which he pronounces "Roh-bairt," in that charming Tuscan way.

There's more wild applause as we return to the mics. For our second tune, I ask Claudio for an old Italian hit from the seventies, "E Penso a Te," by the late Lucio Battisti, one of my favorite singer-songwriters. The recording begins—and it's in a perfectly comfortable key for me. Within a few bars it's clear that I'm more familiar with the tune than Luigina, who quite masterfully covers with a bit of camping it up, which everyone adores.

"E Penso a Te" is one of those wonderfully characteristic builds-to-a-tsunami Italian tunes, and I give this one everything I've got. By the climax, when I get to execute a hair-rising octave jump, I'm pretty sure they can hear me in Grosseto. I'm almost rattling the windows right out of their frames.

People actually get up out of their seats for this, and I have the sudden sense of *arrival* that I've been seeking all these months. I owe it, of course, primarily to Luigina, who's been unfailingly in my corner since I first met her; I'm tempted to lift her right off her feet, but I'm not sure it would suit her dignity.

The contest judges put their heads together and confer for a moment. I feel a tightening in my scalp; a sudden sense of alarm at going too far, too fast. After months of trying to insinuate myself into the ranks of the brucaioli, I've seized on this first glimmering of acceptance and let it go to my head. I've let myself get *pushy*—bellowing like some great ape in the rain forest. The last thing I want to do is brutalize my way into a first prize here tonight. This is a proud people who don't like to be told what to do, especially by some bellicose American wielding a microphone like a bludgeon. Have I set myself up to win a battle, only to lose the war? After striving humbly all these months for success, I find myself, tonight, fearing it.

Third place goes to Riccardo and his duet partner. He's very gracious, smiling as wide as the Chianti hills—*still* working the crowd, even after he's heard the verdict. (I could learn a thing or two from this guy.)

Second place next, and already I'm feeling the pressure of a first-place win . . . but wait a minute, what's happening? People are applauding, Luigina's on her feet, and she's headed toward the front of the room. They've called our names. We're second-place winners.

Which means that the trio of young girls gets the top prize. I mean, I should have seen it coming. I'm a middle-aged bald guy. Anytime, anywhere I come up against beautiful young girls jumping up and down, I'm going to lose. It's one of the immutable laws of the universe. I just never thought it would work to my advantage before.

I squeeze my way through the chair backs and stumble up onto the stage, where Luigina has been presented with a big gold cup affixed with ribbons (blue, green, and yellow, of course). She insists I take it, which is extraordinarily kind of her (though later I realize she probably has an entire room filled with similar trophies). I check out the base, which reads, *Contrada del Bruco 2° Karaokando 2009, 2° Classificato,* and I feel as though I'm holding in my hands real, tangible evidence that I belong.

Afterward, it seems as though everyone wants to shake my hand or buy me a drink or both. Enrico, the silver-haired stal-

wart I met at Giuliano Ghiselli's table a few nights ago, calls
me over to sit with him and his friends awhile. A trio of tawny
young women insist on pouring some prosecco into my prize
cup and watching as I drink from it; it leaks from every seam,
splashing all over my shirtfront, which we all seem to find hilarious. And Antonio, my friend from the bar, hails me and
confers on me the very great honor of sharing his precious
homemade grappa. Which, if it were any stronger, would
have to be registered as a chemical weapon. Seconds after
downing my first mouthful, I can feel all the hair on my chest
just quietly drop off. Even so, I have to swallow the second
mouthful immediately, before it melts right through the plastic cup.

It isn't till later, headed back to Vagliagli in Dario's van,
with the thin beam of his headlamps piercing the voluminous
dark like jouster's lances, that it occurs to me that though I've
had a measure of triumph, it's far from a complete one. I've
opened some doors tonight, but just as many—in fact many
more so—remain firmly in their frames. The full attendance
at tonight's dinner can't have been more than eighty or so brucaioli, from a contrada boasting a membership in the thousands. Aside from Giorgio, none of the officers was there—no
Fabio, no Gianni the capitano, no Gianni the vicario—not
even Francesco, who heads the contrada choir. Possibly news
of my performance will reach some of those ears over the
next few days, as a kind of anecdote or curiosity; but I'm *already* an anecdote and a curiosity. I don't want to diminish the
genuine fellowship that's been offered to me tonight—
I deeply appreciate it, it's like water on parched soil—but it's
not so much arrival as introduction. I still have building to do.

Unfortunately, there's no time. I leave town in two days.

Had the order of this month's events been reversed—commencing with the karaoke night and concluding with dinner with the captain—I might have been able to consolidate my gains in the former, in time to more fully take part in the latter. As it is, I'll have to leave it to fate and hope that when I return in winter the glow of singularity will still linger, and I can pick up where I've left off.

My chief worry, however, is that with the contrada's activity in autumn being diminished, it might be completely moribund a few months hence. Still, there's something about the brucaioli that makes me doubt that a blanket of snow and a bite to the air can suppress completely their fervent social energy and their communitarian zeal. But there's only one way to find out.

D_{OUBT}

. . .

NEXT MORNING AT DARIO'S, I WAKE UP TO FIND RACHEL in the kitchen, preparing breakfast and clearing counters and washing dishes and airing the place out and for all I know tugging the entire Italian peninsula over a few inches to give us better light. And while she's doing all this she looks spectacular, as if she's just waiting her turn to saunter down a runway. Her hair shines and bounces, her eyes sparkle, her clothes are trim and impeccable, and the smile she gives me could stop a jihad in its tracks. She says, "Ciao, Roberto!"—strangely, only my fellow Americans call me Roberto; the Sienese all insist on Robert—and throws her arms around my neck, forgetting that she's still holding a sponge, so that in addition to a hug I get a glob of suds on my neck. I yelp in surprise, and then we both laugh; which is how it always is with Rachel— the time before you're laughing together is measured in milliseconds.

"Sit down, sit down," she insists, as if I've just come in from a hard day's labor instead of just rolling out of bed, and when I obey she sets a plate before me bearing an omelet the size of a yule log. She brings a pot of tea to the table, takes a seat across from me, and starts asking me for all the contrada gossip. I tell her about my big karaoke night, and she hangs on every word as if her own future were riding on the outcome—and then blurts out, "I wish I'd been there!" as though she really, really, really does.

But then she starts asking me for particulars; how so-and-so's job search is going and how somebody else's wife is feeling postsurgery. Most of the people she's mentioning are just names and faces to me, and I feel a sudden sense of unease; it's obvious that Rachel assumes I'm much more intimately connected in the contrada than I am. And why shouldn't she? Haven't I been coming here fairly regularly with just that purpose in mind? And while I'm trying hard to disguise how little I actually know of anyone's state of affairs, she brings out a bag of gifts she's brought for everyone—affectionate, funny tokens that must play off the personality of each recipient because she can't help laughing each time she displays one to me.

A few minutes later Dario wanders downstairs, looking a bit bleary-eyed. He surveys the change in the household and I can tell he's torn between pleasure and apprehension. After all, it *is* nice finally to have the dishes cleared out of the sink—he and I had been eyeing them darkly for the past few days, as though they were uninvited guests who we wished would just leave—but at the same time, he prizes the shaggy randomness of his everyday life, the pleasure to be had in greeting each day on its own terms, and there's none of that to be had in this kind of highly energized atmosphere. Dario is as Dionysian a human being as I've ever met; Rachel, as Apollonian.

I head out to take a stroll, with the excuse that it's my last day and I'd like to say a fond goodbye to the rolling Chianti hills. But really it's to think over this jarring shock I've just suffered. Rachel—who was introduced to the contrada at the same time I was—has dramatically surpassed me, embracing the community and being embraced in return, in a way I can't even begin to imagine. Possibly it's easier for her because she's a beautiful, vivacious woman, while I'm a stocky bald guy.

Yet that didn't stop Roy Moskovitz. By all accounts he was a short, bald, unprepossessing man of middle years, of such ample physicality that he once became wedged in one of the seats of the palchi and remained stuck there till he was discovered later, stranded alone on the Campo in a rainstorm. And yet he adored, and was adored by, all the brucaioli, and a good portion of the rest of Siena too.

What, then, is wrong with me? I try to imagine showing up in the contrada with gifts for everybody, and it just seems awkward and silly. Yet it feels entirely right for Rachel. Possibly this is just a matter of personal style—and personality, period. I have to be accepted on my own terms or not at all. The karaoke night was a good indication of that. I can do this in my own way.

I have to keep in mind something Dario told me the last time I experienced a degree of frustration. He said, "Rob, you're an American, you're gay, and you're a writer. None of those are things the Sienese see a lot of." The implication being that any one of those attributes would've been an obstacle to easy acceptance; but all three in one package?

In the piazza a woman stops and asks me if it's true that Rachel has arrived, and I tell her indeed it is. I've never actually spoken to this person before, nor she to me, but it's clear now that she's well enough aware of my identity to know I'll be able to tell her about Rachel. The unsettled feeling comes over me again as I recall that not only is Rachel a favorite among the contrada; she's also well beloved here in Vagliagli. And though I've stayed here often, I know only a handful of the villagers by name, and none of them extraordinarily well.

There's something unnerving about being confronted with the fact of someone who shares your ambitions but pursues them with greater energy, positivity, and success. Maybe it's not about being American or gay or a writer. Maybe it's about being a tentative, timid, unyielding kind of guy, self-obsessed but not self-confident, drawn to light and joy while privately nursing drear and dourness. Maybe I'm just not a people person. Maybe I'm just not *likable*. Not everyone can be. It's not the end of the freakin' world.

And people can change. Maybe the next time I come here, I can make a concerted effort to be less inner-directed, more open to the views and experiences of other people. Peggy, the American brucaiola, said the way to gain entry into the contrada was to "just be here." But there's more to "just being here" than simply occupying a space. I think I'm beginning to get that now.

When I began this journey, I knew there'd be some difficulties along the way, but I presumed they would be mainly tactical: travel problems, the language barrier. I didn't realize I'd find myself facing a complete top-down reconstruction of my entire character.

But if that's what it takes, that's what I'll do.

PART FIVE

*W*inter · 2010

...

WARMING
TRENDS

"*THE PALIO IS DEAD*"

. . .

⚒ I'M READY FOR A RENEWED ASSAULT ON THE BASTIONS of the Bruco, but it's the dead of February. What, I wonder, constitutes the life of the contrada in the bleakest weeks of the year? Most of the brucaioli who have posted on Facebook during the past month have mentioned only the inclement weather—especially a vicious blizzard that descended on them in the days before I'm set to return.

When I arrive, the snow remains piled high in some places but bleeds away in others. It's one of those peculiar days where the temperature in the shade is subarctic, but just a few steps into the sun and you're compelled to remove your scarf and unbutton your collar. I have to cover a lot of ground on my journey from the airport in Bologna, through the Florence train station, to the terminal at Siena, and by the time I get there I feel as though I've been frozen, thawed, and frozen again about a dozen times over, like a supermarket fish stick.

Dario meets me at the train station, bearing a box of organic pici from the warehouse that he's earmarked for our dinner. But as we arrive in Vagliagli he comes up with an idea: rather than cook it at home and burden ourselves with the trouble of laying a table and clearing it away afterward (and with no Rachel around to do it for us), he pulls up to Osteria L'Antico Detto, just thirty seconds down the road from his place. It's a weeknight in February, so business there is bound to be slow; he'll ask Giovanna if she'd mind cooking the pasta for us.

Giovanna wouldn't mind at all. In fact, she seems glad of the company, and after she sets the pot boiling she comes out and lights a cigarette and sits down to chat. Her young waiter, Dani, lingers on the sidelines, jumping to attention whenever Giovanna tosses him an order.

Giovanna is a handsome, athletic-looking woman with fine cheekbones and sand-colored hair she wears pulled back from her face. She also speaks very briskly, so I have difficulty keeping the thread of her conversation. Occasionally she pauses to take a drag off her cigarette and I have a chance to catch up, but as soon as she starts in again I'm left gasping.

Perhaps inevitably, talk soon turns to the Palio. I hadn't known it before, but Giovanna is Sienese—from the Panther contrada, which I still hold in esteem and affection after its hospitality to me last August. But unlike Dario, Giovanna isn't enamored of the great annual rite in the Piazza del Campo.

She keeps saying *"È morto il Palio"*—"The Palio is dead." She and Dario argue the point for a while, not back and forth but overlapping each other, as Italians sometimes will, so that at first I can't get a sense of what she means; but eventually Dario sits back and sighs and lets her rail on for a bit, and I get a gist of where she's coming from.

Basically, she feels that the Palio has become a spectacle— no longer a rite for the Sienese but a show put on for visitors and gawkers. This is astonishing to me, because to my eyes—

and admittedly I'm one of the gawkers—everything about the Palio is deeply, invincibly authentic. There's no corporate sponsorship, no crass commercialization; you have to look hard even to spot a TV camera. As for tourists—again, admittedly I am one; but ask any tourist how catered to he feels in Siena at Palio time, when the *cittadini* surge forcefully through the streets of their city like blood pumping through vital arteries, knocking visitors aside like stray bacteria. It's nothing at all like, say, Florence, where you have to hire a bloodhound to track down an actual Florentine.

As I consider this, Dario is taking his turn at bat. "You can't say the Palio is dead," he insists. "You can say it's changed—and it has, of course it has; whether for good or ill, that's a matter of opinion. But you can't say it's *died*. As long as there is turf laid in the piazza every summer and ten contrade send out horses to race, the Palio lives."

Giovanna keeps waving her cigarette in response, as though she can simply scatter Dario's logic in midair, the way you'd flap away a bad smell. It's at this point that Michele comes in, and Giovanna takes the opportunity to go to the kitchen and dish up the pici.

Michele doesn't stay long enough for a drink, which is saying something; but he apparently has a driver's test the next day and is wisely playing it safe. (His license was once confiscated when he was on his way to a victory dinner in the Porcupine. He says it's a good thing he was pulled over while going *to* the dinner instead of *from;* otherwise they'd also have taken his car, his house, his mother, and his girlfriend.) (I ought to add that *of course* he went on to the dinner anyway, after having consigned his car keys to the carabinieri.) After he leaves we tuck into our pici, and Giovanna lights a new cigarette. If I thought Michele's cameo appearance would serve as a palate cleanser, prefacing a new topic of conversation, I was wrong, because Dario and Giovanna immediately pick up where they left off.

A few minutes later someone else comes through the door, and wouldn't you know it, it's another Sienese—a worldly-looking man of middle years named Angelo, better known by his tongue-twisting nickname, Gnagno (pronounced *NYAHN-nyoh*), who's introduced to me as being of the Unicorn. (When you're introduced in America, your occupation follows your name—in Siena, it's your contrada affiliation.)

Gnagno joins the conversation, but with less intensity than Giovanna and Dario (later I'll learn that he's still a bit shell-shocked from August, when the Unicorn's great rival the Owl won its first Palio in twenty years). As their talk gets faster and more furious, I lose all track of it. It's like one of those trios in a Mozart opera where everyone tells the audience what they're thinking, only you can't really understand because they're all singing at the same time, and also it's in Italian. And in fact it's as though I'm watching a small-scale production of *Don Giovanni,* with Dario crooning a gently urgent tune, trying to seduce the others into taking his view; Giovanna, à la Donna Elvira, keeps furiously running up the scale, starting with a growl and ending on an aggrieved trill; and Gnagno bounces merrily between them, like a witty Leporello.

And this is when it hits me: the wine, the smoke, the intensity of the emotions, the music of the language . . . *I'm back*. The weather may be grim, the street life fallow, but Tuscany remains Tuscany, and heat and vitality are never in short supply.

Giovanna ducks to the kitchen for a moment, returning with sliced steak for us, served with a spinach-Parmesan mold; it's aromatic and colorful and completely delicious. Dani refills our glasses, and while Giovanna lights yet another cigarette, as deliberately as if she were igniting a cannon, Dani smiles at me, and I smile back.

"Crazy," I say, nodding my head at the three others. Then, thinking he might misunderstand me, I add, "Crazy *wonderful*."

He pulls up a chair. "I know. I always think so too."

"But you must be used to it by now."

He shakes his head. "I haven't been here long enough."

"You're not a native, then?"

It turns out he's not. He comes from Turin but has landed in Chianti by way of Ireland, China, and—no kidding—Tennessee.

"What brought you here, then?" I ask.

"A girlfriend. That's how I know the Sienese. She's from there." He pauses only briefly before adding, "Snail," as though I would of course need to know her contrada.

"They're a very different kind of people, aren't they?"

"It's a strange city," he says. "Stranger to me than China . . . stranger even than Tennessee." I have to laugh at that. "But I'm so jealous of my girlfriend, because to her it's *not* strange. To her it's normal."

I sense a kindred spirit, and further discussion reveals that in fact he, like me, finds himself wildly attracted to the city's close-knit communities and envious of those born into them. I tell him I hope to earn my way into the Caterpillar contrada, and he wishes me luck, in a way that manages to mix earnest good wishes with a little dollop of *You'll need it*.

When he gets up to clear our plates, he's so stealthy that Giovanna, now deeply engrossed in her conversation—and so shrouded by smoke she can barely see; she looks like the Oracle of Delphi—doesn't notice him go. And when Dario, attempting to convince her that the Palio and its traditions are as solid as ever, uses me as an example—"That's what brings Rob over here so often; he sees their value and has come to study and understand them"—Giovanna, clearly unaware that I'm now listening to every word, snorts in derision and says, quite clearly, "Rob appalls me."

Immediately my face burns, and I feel a prickle of shame creep over me. I feel as though I've been found out—Giovanna has taken my measure and found me wanting: a tourist, an interloper, a poseur. I have a horrified moment in which I wonder how many other people have looked at me and reached the same conclusion.

But after another moment's reflection, I regain some composure. After all, Giovanna has just cooked me an absolutely lovely dinner and waved away Dario's wallet when he had the temerity to produce it, which means that in addition to being delicious it was a gift; so if she wants to find me appalling, I'm more than willing to grant her the privilege. Also, I'm sufficiently familiar with the Tuscan character to know that declarations made in the heat of argument are seldom deeply felt. And in fact twenty minutes later—when we've moved on to some after-dinner shots of grappa—she sits by my side and, her mood now lightened by a good smoke and a rousing argument (two great Tuscan pleasures), shows me some photos stored on her cellphone. They're of a recent Panther victory, which was apparently made all the sweeter by the radio announcer having first called the race for Eagle, the Panther's bitter enemy—only to have a video replay alter the verdict for the Panther. This kind of thing—not only winning but tearing the victory away from your already celebrating rival—is, for a Sienese, the purest joy imaginable. And in fact Giovanna mentions that this was, in her opinion, the victory of the century.

"I wasn't there," she says. "I was at a wedding, so at first I heard only that the Eagle had won. I cried all through the ceremony. Then afterward—well, you can imagine how I felt when I heard the news!" She's beaming, showing me photo after photo of the festivities that followed.

I tell her, "Giovanna, look at what you're doing. You've just been saying 'The Palio is dead,' but here you are sharing with me this extraordinary moment in your life, and *it's a Palio*." She gives me a look—one that I encounter often in these parts—that clearly conveys, *What has that got to do with it?* There are obviously subtleties at work here that I don't—and may never—understand.

It's become rather clear that any disdain Giovanna feels for me is due to my having signed my soul over to the Caterpillar without even getting to know the alternatives. Whatever the case, one more shot of grappa is poured. Dani and I go back to discussing the Sienese. I say, with the passionate conviction that only the truly visionary or the truly drunk can summon forth, "In every society, there are frictions, passions, turbulent emotions—yet here they're organized." Actually, the word I used is *sistemati*—which doesn't have an exact English analogue. It means not merely organized but arranged—managed. It's a difficult word for an American to comprehend in all its nuances. I don't think I really got it myself till I came to Siena.

Eventually I find myself at the door with Dario, donning my coat and saying goodbye to Giovanna and Dani and Gnagno. I'm a bit unsteady on my feet, but I wouldn't have said no to another grappa—or even one after that. Never mind that it would be wrong and evil and harmful to my future prospects; I'm feeling . . . *headlong*. Happy to be back and contemptuous of all restraint.

And thus ready for my return to the contrada, tomorrow night.

Intestinal Fortitude

. . .

I've barely recovered—from either the jet lag or the grappa—yet I find myself back in Società L'Alba for another Dinner with the Captain. It is, I learn, the last such; I thought it was an ongoing series, but no, it's been a special program, and tonight Gianni retires from his hosting duties. It's time for him to turn his attention to the coming Palio.

The menu for the night comes as a surprise: it's heavy on tripe, which is something you just don't see in America, given our general squeamishness. But this is one of the ways in which I feel definitely more European than Yank; I can't gobble up the stuff fast enough. Not only is it thoroughly delicious, it's a matter of principle. Any responsible carnivore will consume *everything* edible on an animal; to do any less is wasteful, disrespectful, and—dare I say it?—unnatural.

As if the tripe weren't enough, there's a risotto made with lampredotto, a Tuscan specialty. Tripe comes from the first three chambers of the cow's stomach; lampredotto from the fourth. It has a wonderfully pungent flavor, and I'm an immediate fan. Dario tells me that there are lampredotto vendors who ply their wares in carts between Siena and Florence, serving the delicacy on slabs of bread.

I'm seated at a table with some of Dario's friends—Luigi, Luciano, Katia. I feel much more at ease around them than I used to, and the feeling seems increasingly reciprocal. Just across the table from me is Daniele, a very tall, very handsome, casually elegant type whose clothes look as though they were sewn onto his body. It doesn't surprise me to learn that he's from Milan. He's here because he married a brucaiola—though she seems to be seated elsewhere. Very nice guy, though I wonder that I seem suddenly to be talking to so many non-Sienese. Maybe Giovanna has a point; maybe the incursion of people like Daniele and me has permanently altered the whole tone of contrada life, and by extension the Palio.

While I'm stewing over this, Gianni seems to be enjoying himself tremendously, possibly from relief at knowing that this is the last dinner he'll have to host. All his reserve has melted away; he's relaxed, funny, charming. I'm glad for him; he deserves one night of pure pleasure in the spotlight, because the weeks and months ahead are going to be grueling.

Already, there's a hint of winter exhaustion hanging over the room and a kind of valedictory air to the dinner, as though afterward we're all going to go home, climb under the covers, and hibernate till spring. That's not really an option for me. I'm here for only a limited time, I have to make the most of it. I don't want to seem like a voyeur—though I sometimes feel like one—but observation is the first step to integration. Otherwise I'll remain a strange man in a strange land. And so the next day, despite a steady downpour, I have Dario drop me back in Siena.

The rain doesn't let up all day, so that I'm driven to take refuge in one after another of the city's museums, churches, and civic buildings; none of which lacks beauty or interest, but I've seen them all before. What I've come for is *life*—the present tense, the vital, urgent, turbulent surge forward; the communal experience, so passionate in all its particulars, that differentiates this city, these people, from any I've ever encountered elsewhere. What I've come for is to tap the wellspring of Sienese-ness that I've missed in my American life. What I've come for is to drench myself in Siena; and instead Siena is drenching me with rain.

But I'm not giving up; I still have Giovanna in my back pocket. She offered to take me around the Panther today—perhaps with the intention of making me regret my quick adoption of the Caterpillar—but we didn't really settle on when. Alas, a few minutes later I receive a text; she has to cancel. Her little dog has died.

These unhappy tidings set a pall over the day—a day that's worked rather hard at being appalling. Cold, gray, wet, and lonely; and now tinged with bereavement. I look at my watch; it's not even close to cocktail hour—but what the hell. In such circumstances as these, a glass of wine is medicinal.

I don't want to have it on the Campo, however. I'll see only tourists. I'll go to the nameless bar in the Bruco, and even if no one else is there, *I* will be.

The rain is still falling with depressing steadiness; it's not exactly violent—that would be preferable, because a violent storm would eventually exhaust itself. My boots hold out against the onslaught, but my glasses fog and my pants legs dampen. I've made it nearly to the bar when I spot Nikke, the clothier, seated in his shop reading a newspaper. I decide to duck in and say hello, and give myself a brief respite from the rain.

"Ciao, Nikke," I say, and he looks up with a grin and gestures for me to sit, never mind how wet I am. The first time I met him, when I stopped into his store and grandly introduced myself as an American Palio enthusiast and a dues-paying Protector of the Caterpillar, his welcome wasn't quite so ready; in fact, he regarded me with something just a hair shy of suspicion and kept me standing in his doorway for the better part of half an hour. But gradually his reserve melted away; possibly the genuineness of my interest (or the endearing clumsiness of my Italian) put him off his guard. By the time I took my leave of him he was so firmly one of my well-wishers that he got up and shook my hand and walked me out, and seemed almost ready to follow me back up the street—as a kind of protector's protector. Saint Catherine once said, "If there are people in the world whom you can win over with love, they are the Sienese."

Now, back in Nikke's store, I nod my head toward the bleak weather beyond the window and say, "Sorry you left Rome now?" Nikke is a native Sienese, but he lived in Rome for forty years, returning to his hometown only at sixty. He shrugs and says, "It rains in Rome too"—clearly implying that when it rains in Rome it's worse, because . . . well, you're in Rome. *Campanilismo* is an Italian term, derived from the word *campanile,* or bell tower, that describes the average Italian's passionate devotion to his own city, town, or region— for which said bell tower serves as a symbol. Tuscans are especially prone to campanilismo, not only in reference to faraway cities like Rome but to other Tuscan towns just a few miles up the road. And of course the Sienese practice campanilismo on an even more localized scale, with fierce rivalries between the seventeen contrade. Something else: passionate allegiance to your own campanile goes hand in hand with disparaging everyone else's. Pisa seems to take the brunt of this; there's an old saying known to every Tuscan, *Meglio avere un morto in casa che un Pisano alla porta*—"Better a corpse in your house than a Pisano on your doorstep."

As Nikke and I continue to chat about nothing much in particular, I realize that this is in fact a very Sienese thing to do: stop and pass the time of day. I've done it only to get out of the rain for a few minutes, but it doesn't matter. For a brief moment, without even realizing it, I've fallen into the pattern of life here; instead of bolting around with my eyes bugging out, calling attention to myself, I've quietly, unthinkingly blended in.

I feel a little glow of pride in my breast as I shake Nikke's hand and depart. I feel almost native.

Forget about the glass of wine . . . *this* is the fix I needed.

*F*ISH OUT of *WATER*

. . .

MY WINTER SOJOURN AMONG THE CATERPILLAR—MARKED by stillness, marred by rain, but made memorable by brief encounters and small moments that might have passed unnoticed at a more bustling time of year—is drawing to an end. By sheer good fortune, there's another dinner at the Società a few days before I depart, so I can once again view the brucaioli in the aggregate and say my goodbyes. I'm expecting another quiet, amiable evening like Gianni's final Dinner with the Captain.

In fact, it proves to be something entirely different. Lent has begun, so this Friday repast is to be all seafood, and it's to be prepared by the young people of the contrada—the teens and twentysomethings. The principal chef seems to be Alessio, nicknamed Ciancha because he's the son of Cianchino, the jockey who ended the Bruco's long losing streak in 1996 and thus became an instant hero. Cianchino responded by having his sons baptized in the contrada, and Alessio certainly appears at home here. A dark-eyed, jet-haired young man, he manages somehow to give off an aura of both frenetic energy and laserlike focus. He doesn't so much exit the kitchen as burst out of it, to work the crowd or grab a quick smoke, or to make some announcement in so heightened a state of excitement that I can't understand a word of it.

When I was a kid, my dad bought me an LP record called *501 Sound Effects,* and for some reason I loved to just sit with my eyes closed and play it all the way through. The sounds emanating from the kitchen remind me a little of that now. I expect at any moment a hail of pots and pans to erupt from the doorway, or a small mushroom cloud. At intervals, young people in smocks and aprons come rocketing out. The first course is late, but there seems to be no apprehension or impatience; people—Dario and I included—just keep opening more bottles of wine, with the result that the mood in the place keeps getting livelier and happier. Suddenly, without warning, the February doldrums begin to take on the character of sun-dazzled July.

When the food finally appears, it's impeccably prepared, beautifully plated, and disorientingly flavorful. Calamari bruschette, steamed mussels in a garlic broth, gnocchi with shrimp and crab, delicately poached sea bass. While we're feasting, Alessio's continued reappearances in the dining room prompt me to wonder about his father, whom I haven't yet met; how many Palii, exactly, did Cianchino ride for the Caterpillar over the course of his career?

It's an obvious enough question from a newcomer, but I'm surprised by how eagerly the brucaioli take it up. This is the kind of thing they live for. No one seems to have an indisputable answer at his fingertips, so they spend the next several minutes rifling through their memories and tallying up the races—sometimes pausing to dispute an assertion or argue that someone's gotten the year wrong. Eventually the answer is determined: eight—possibly nine, if you count July 1996, when he broke his leg in the *prova generale* before the race. (Nothing is ever clear-cut about the Palio. Which is part of its appeal.)

With the food now prepared and served, the kitchen staff are at their ease, and though their demeanor up to now can't exactly be called efficient (word leaks out that they ran a Crab Palio on the countertop before cooking up the crustaceans), the successful completion of their task comes as such a happy release to them that they basically degenerate into anarchy. I find myself envying them, remembering the way everything at that age—every accomplishment, every pitfall, heartbreak, and triumph—is so heightened that it feels cataclysmic. What's coming from the kitchen now is the sound of pure, untrammeled joy. Part of the proceeds from tonight's dinner goes to a fund for Gianni's hoped-for fourth victory—not unprecedented for a captain, but extremely rare—and when I slip into the kitchen to scope out what's going on, Alessio and the others all have their arms around one another and are throatily singing, "We will hang it once more"—meaning the prize banner.

Eventually people begin wafting away from the dinner tables and congregating in the bar, which is where Dario introduces me to Claudio Bani, who is the contrada's barbaresco—a position of inexpressible importance that Bani has held for an incredible seventeen years. His chief responsibility is that of groom to the horse during the days of the Palio, though in that capacity he's augmented by an exceptional horse whisperer from Rome called Er Mutanda (literally, "the underwear"—how he earned this nickname isn't explained, and frankly I'm fine with that). But during the remainder of the year the barbaresco is equally preoccupied, traveling about the country to follow the training and development of the horses that will be offered for consideration for the Palio. The advice of the *barbareschi* and the captain's aides, the *mangini,* will be crucial in determining which mounts make the cut.

Because of these demands, the barbaresco is a rare sight in the contrada; he's almost always on the road, and during the days of the Palio he's perpetually at the stable with the horse, thereby missing all the dinners and the feasts. Bani, however, looks quite at peace with this life of near isolation. Lean, taut, and completely bald though still appearing quite youthful (I'd guess him to be in his very early forties), he seems tremendously self-contained; he barely moves a muscle but exudes power and confidence. I suppose these are all traits necessary in the handling of highly strung horses, and indeed it's hard, after chatting with Bani for just a few minutes, to imagine a scenario in which he'd rush to judgment or overreact.

As if to demonstrate this, the young kitchen staff—now almost wild over their big success tonight—descend on the bar like a squadron of paratroopers. There's shouting, shoving, singing, and a surprising amount of leaping about. But no one seems to mind much, least of all Bani, who barely acknowledges the sudden influx. He's telling us which were the most exceptional horses he's handled in his nearly two decades on the job. "Vai Go was the most surprising to me," he says; later I'll learn that this was a horse who almost won scosso (riderless) in 2004. "I had no idea he was so powerful."

"What about Elisir?" I ask. "He took everyone by surprise, didn't he?"

Bani allows the most muted smile to cross his lips. "Not me. I knew from the start what Elisir could do, and I knew when his time had come." Just beyond us, Alessio and some of the others have started taking packages of snack foods from the display cases and smashing them underfoot. Crisps, chips, and pretzels are flying everywhere; it's as though someone stepped on a land mine set by Keebler Elves. "Urban, on the other hand," Bani continues, completely unfazed and recalling a horse ridden by Trecciolino in July 2002, "I had much greater expectations for him . . . ."

The level of destruction keeps mounting, and I can't help feeling a bit on my guard. I'm in a crowded bar, hemmed in by dozens of people, and there's a small-scale riot going on just a few steps away. But everyone else here looks either unconcerned or affectionately amused, so I try to be cool—especially since Bani, in response to an inquiry from Dario, has become even more introspective; the more chaotic things get all around him, the more serene and thoughtful he appears to become. "It can be a very lonely existence, yes," he says. "A barbaresco is never really off duty. Any kind of social life is next to impossible, never mind a relationship . . . still, it's my choice to do this, and though I've done it for seventeen years, I don't feel in any way that I've reached my limit. I can't imagine giving it up. It's a calling as much as a job."

At this point, someone bursts a bag of mixed nuts over my head, and a little shower of pecans and almonds cascades down past my collar. (I'll be shaking them out for the rest of the night, and when I awaken tomorrow morning I'll find an entire cashew sitting primly on the pillow next to me. And one week later, back home in Chicago, I'll have to stop while walking the dogs because of what I think is a pebble in my shoe, but when I shake it out I'll see that it's a pistachio.)

Now, you'd think that this would alarm me; it's the first

hint of the rowdiness in the bar turning actually violent. Yet it's also so absurd. I've been attacked with a bag of snacks; more salted than assaulted. It almost feels like an ironic welcome. And sure enough, as I look over my shoulder, I can see that I'm not the only one being preyed on in this manner—and that all the victims are taking it with giddy good humor. In a way, it feels as much a rite of passage as winning the karaoke trophy with Luigina.

And suddenly I know innately that no one is in any peril here tonight. This is just another example of high spirits, driven by excitement and fraternity, by testosterone and Chianti Classico. In another place, such a combination might lead to something lethal; but this is Siena—everything is structured, everything is channeled, everything is sistemati. Even as I'm thinking this, I notice that one of the revelers has taken up a broom and begun sweeping up after his friends, who are still busily bursting snack packs. This kind of carousing is allowed and even smiled upon, because everyone here knows what the boundaries are; this is their place—their collective home—and they can be utterly themselves here, never mind how extreme the behavior that results. But for the same reason, they respect the place; they honor it and they preserve it. So yes, go crazy, tear up the joint, bash it to bits. You know where the broom and dustpan are.

By the end of the night the bar is looking pretty much restored to order. I'm also fairly certain someone is happily settling up for the damaged inventory, too—probably the perpetrators themselves or their fathers. If there's a harsh word to be said over any of this, I'm not hearing it. In fact, it appears quite the opposite: everyone is leaving with smiles and laughter.

I'm feeling pretty good myself, but on the way home I become aware of a small, sharp pain in one of my lower teeth. Probably the wine dulled it a bit so that I didn't feel it until now. In which case, a little *more* wine when we get back to Vagliagli ought to dull it enough to let me sleep. If it's still there in the morning, I'll worry about it then.

RECTIFIED

. . .

⚕ THE NEXT DAY THE PAIN IS WORSE; I CAN BARELY TOUCH the affected area with my tongue, and my face has a slightly swollen aspect.

"I think I might have cracked a tooth," I say.

"How is that possible at a seafood dinner?" Dario asks, quite reasonably.

"Maybe I bit down on a mussel shell or something. I don't remember."

"Would some hot tea help?"

The hot tea doesn't help.

"Ow, ow, ow!" I wail as the steaming brew scalds the tooth's tender nerves.

"You should go and see Fabio," Dario says.

"Fabio? The rector?"

"He's a dentist," Dario explains.

To me, it's always seemed as though being rector of the Caterpillar must be a full-time job. It had completely slipped my mind that he has another career alongside it.

"I'll give him a ring, see if he can fit you in," Dario offers. "If he can, I'll give you a lift to Siena."

Fabio's office is located in Piazza Gramsci, not far from the

Siena bus station, a place I've come to know well. "Bus station" has a rather seedy connation in the United States, but the station in Siena is actually a very pleasant spot. The ticket office is below ground, so all that's on the surface is the buses, just two or three at a time; this is, remember, a very small city. I sometimes bring my lunch here and sit and watch the travelers come and go.

There are gently waving trees across the way, and just over the rooftops you can spy the imposing edifice of the Basilica of San Domenico, which houses some of the remains of Saint Catherine—her head and thumb, to be precise. (The rest of her is interred in Rome.)

The story goes that the Sienese, believing that Catherine would prefer to be laid to rest in her own city but knowing they couldn't smuggle her entire body out of the capital, settled on taking only her head. When, despite this precaution, Roman guards stopped them and commanded them to open their sack, what they found there was a mound of rose petals. Once safely beyond the walls of the city, the faithful reopened the sack and looked again; Catherine's head had been restored. Relic and miracle, all in one package.

Catherine was a towering figure, not just for the Sienese but for all of Europe, and in fact she remains so (she's the patron saint of both the city and the continent). She had that medieval bent for self-mortification—hair shirts, autoflagellation, sleeping with a stone for a pillow. Yet she was also a relentless firebrand, a champion of the poor and a protofeminist in the truest sense; she wrote hectoring letters to just about everyone—kings, dukes, mercenaries—she even badgered the pope on matters both spiritual and temporal. She'd probably have made a spectacularly awful dinner guest. No one else would've been able to get a word in. Also, she famously didn't eat. In her latter days she even tried to give up water, preferring to drink the pus of the afflicted. Which frankly I prefer not to serve in my house.

Fabio's office is located in one of those wonderful old fortresslike buildings you find only in Europe, with a great carved door big enough to admit a woolly mammoth. Inside there are a grand staircase and a cage elevator, like something out of a Vincente Minnelli movie. Caramel-colored light pours in from a sky-high window.

Fabio has promised to try to fit me in between his scheduled appointments, so I have to wait on his convenience. In the waiting room there are magazines and newspapers on hand, but my tooth hurts too much to allow the requisite concentration for reading in Italian. I take refuge in my iPod, fully aware of how distressingly American this makes me look. A mitigating factor, if anyone but knew it, is that I'm not listening to some mind-numbing pop music; I'm actually tuned in to a podcast, *12 Byzantine Rulers* by the historian Lars Brownworth. In this episode he's talking about the reign of the Emperor Justinian, and in particular his commission of the Hagia Sophia church in Constantinople, in its time the most spectacular building in the world (and still a jaw-dropper today). Even more astonishing is that it was built in just five years, ten months, and four days from the laying of the first stone—which Brownworth cannily compares to the much later edifices of Westminster Cathedral (thirty-three years to build), Notre Dame (more than a hundred), and the Duomo in Florence (two hundred thirty). What occurs to me instantly, of course, is that the Duomo of Siena is *still* unfinished after eight hundred years; there's an entire nave of which only one wall has been erected. Granted, its construction was halted in 1348 by the Black Death, which pretty much decimated the workforce for the next few generations. And then those pushy Florentines took over the city (and its purse strings), which basically meant forget about it.

Eventually—and sooner than I'd thought; the Emperor Justinian hasn't even died yet—I'm summoned from the reception area into a chair, and Fabio appears in a white smock, beaming quiet authority.

"Thank you for seeing me on such short notice," I say. "I think I broke a tooth."

"Let's have a look," he says, and as he's peering into my mouth I realize that he has almost exactly the eyes of Albert Einstein—there's the same quality of empathic wisdom in them. Ancient eyes, which you can easily miss because he's otherwise so youthful.

After a bit of prodding, Fabio reaches in with some tweezerlike instruments and removes a small fish bone. "This was lodged in your gum," he says; "that's what caused the pain and the swelling. The tooth itself is sound."

This is of course a relief, but I also feel a little foolish. It seems somehow unmanly that something so tiny—the bone is scarcely more than a filament, barely visible in the light—could so disable me.

And just like that, I'm out of the chair again. I wasn't even there long enough to warm the seat. I follow Fabio into his office, whose walls are a kind of pale salmon, perhaps the better to set off the yellow, blue, and green of the Bruco artifacts around the room, which include barberi balls, framed prints, a miniature pennant, ceramic pieces, and carved caterpillars.

It's a little temple to the Caterpillar, here in the heart of the Porcupine.

"Thanks for taking the time to see me," I say, trying to prolong the encounter. "I didn't realize you were so busy. It surprises me, actually. I thought being rector of the Bruco was a full-time job."

He smiles. "It's not so bad as that."

"It must be very demanding."

"I suppose it is. It doesn't feel that way. Actually, I enjoy it."

"It shows. I think people appreciate it, too. I've heard some of them say, only half jokingly, that you should be rector for life."

He chuckles. "Well, that's very generous. But I don't think it's such a good idea. This is a very good time in the contrada, very constructive and positive. But I don't want them to be stuck with me when the time comes for a change, as it always does. I'm willing to continue serving for as long as I'm useful, but there's a reason for the two-year election cycle. When the time comes for fresh blood, I'll be happy to step aside."

"Would you ever become captain instead?" Another rumor I've heard.

"No, I think not; I don't have the knowledge of horses required. Also, the captain is concerned almost exclusively with the Palio—negotiating, laying the groundwork, doing whatever is necessary to win. Which is, of course, of vital importance. But I prefer to devote myself to the everyday affairs of the contrada."

"Well, I have to compliment you on that. You realize that's why I'm here, don't you? When I first came to Siena, I instantly became a Palio enthusiast. But the more I studied and learned, the more the Palio, for all its drama and excitement, became a secondary consideration. It's the life of the contrada that's the real phenomenon here. To me, it's an ideal society. Everyone comes together, everyone belongs, everyone has such pride. I envy that. It must be wonderful to be part of it."

He's nodding as I speak, as though appreciating the fact that I really do *get* it. Everyone likes to have his work acknowledged, and by all accounts Fabio has worked creditably hard to turn the Caterpillar around after several moribund decades. Gianni's success at winning Palii has of course been of vital importance, as well. It's really been my good fortune to have found an entrée into this particular contrada at this particular time. It's almost certainly the happiest and best run in the whole city. I occasionally hear stories about other contrade's assemblies ending with people throwing punches or hurling chairs; and even in the Caterpillar, things were much more fractious during the long losing streak before 1996. But now, with three victories in five years, they're basking in success.

Though on second thought, it isn't luck that brought me here. If what I'd first seen of the brucaioli had been tense and unruly, I'd never have bothered exploring their way of life at all. I'm here solely because of the particular magic that they, and only they, can conjure at this specific moment in time. If luck is involved at all, it's not that I was lucky to have found the Caterpillar; it's that the Caterpillar was here to be found.

My chat with Fabio has now become almost social; in fact, his assistant comes in and offers me an espresso. I accept but drink it down in one gulp; it's the middle of a busy workday morning, and Fabio has professional duties to attend to. I

know this only by the bustle of activity that I can sense beyond his office door; he himself shows no sign of anxiety or
hurry or impatience. It occurs to me that this must be his true
gift as rector: the ability to *listen*. How often have you heard
that said about a great leader? "He/she made me feel like the
only other person in the room." Well, in this case I really *am*
the only person in the room; but I'm sure as hell not the only
other person in his office.

After thanking him for his time and heading back out to
the street, I feel a kind of exhilaration—as though the wind is
at my back. And it's not just the sudden alleviation of my
toothache. It's a bright, clear morning, and the whole day is
open before me. I start walking and find myself inexorably
drawn to the Caterpillar district. Stricken by a sudden pang of
hunger, I stop into the fruit shop run by Mario, a lifelong brucaiolo, and buy a clementine. A tall, lanky man of middle age
with an aristocratic mien, Mario is a good source of information on the life of the Bruco, especially given that his shop is
in the very heart of the contrada, just yards from the grotto
containing the sculpture of both the rampant caterpillar and
the heroic Barbicone.

As I get my citrus fix, he and I chat, and I find myself having a kind of replay of my talk with Fabio. "The thing about
the Bruco," he says, "is that it has two aspects. Because, you
see, Siena is made up of seventeen small, independent states;
each contrada is its own sovereign entity, governed by its inhabitants. Yet each contrada is also an extended family. All
the *bambini* of the Bruco are my nieces and nephews; anyone
you meet here will say the same. It's why we have no drugs
here, no delinquency."

He tells me I would see this family aspect most clearly il-

lustrated if I could witness one of the big rites of passage—
a baptism, a wedding, a funeral. But the contrada also works
in quieter, less showy ways; for example, lending support to
young people who leave home for the first time or to those
who fall into economic distress. "Two aspects," Mario concludes, "but only one nature."

I find myself thinking back to last year's August Palio,
when the Tower contrada extracted one of the most desired
horses. Rather than react with the usual burst of near-violent
ecstasy, they collected the mount in complete silence and led
it out of the Campo in quiet dignity. Only later did we learn
that this was a gesture of respect to the family of the boy who
had just died. Now I realize it was more than a gesture; all
those torraioli in the Campo that day, in their dozens if not
hundreds, *were* the boy's family, in a very real sense.

It's a disorienting epiphany; it makes me aware of the
magnitude of the task I've set myself. How can I ever fully
comprehend the breadth and depth, much less the intricacies
and nuances, of life in a contrada, especially when I can con-
trive to be here only a handful of times during the year? I
don't have the resources to live in Siena for any extended
time.

My sails, so recently billowed, now droop a little. I feel
suddenly like a tourist again. I depart Siena the next day,
wondering if I'll ever remotely get it right.

PART SIX

Spring · *2010*

· · ·

WINNERS/
LOSERS

*A*SHEN

...

JUST DAYS BEFORE I'M DUE TO RETURN TO SIENA FOR my next visit, a volcano with the cat-runs-across-the-keyboard name of Eyjafjallajökull erupts in Iceland, vomiting up such a quantity of ash and grit into the atmosphere that flights across Europe are summarily canceled; almost the entire continent is grounded. Rachel, who's also heading back, departed just hours before the blast, and it's a few days before I hear from Dario that she's arrived safely—after having to abandon air travel somewhere along the way and complete the journey by boat. Again, she's utterly outdone me. My November walk from Vagliagli to Porta Ovile seems quite literally pedestrian next to her epic trawl over earth and water, through air and fire—epic *and* elemental, then—to reach the sweet haven of Società L'Alba. My journey took four hours; hers, a compressed geologic age. I picture her at the prow of some wave-tossed vessel, the wind whipping her hair dramatically behind her as she peers through hot rain and stinging ash for her first glimpse of the Italian peninsula. As compared to me kicking through autumn leaves in my boots and my anorak, my backpack filled with snacks.

I try to take comfort in discomfort; that is, in the pain I'm currently suffering due to the onset of shingles. About a week ago, a few itchy welts erupted on my flank, which I assumed must be insect bites. I blamed the dogs for having dragged some pernicious thing with mandibles into the house and deposited it on the couch (we have three dogs; *you* try to keep them off the furniture). But calamine lotion didn't ease the inflammation, and within a few days I had an ugly stripe of red swooping up my side into my upper back—and the itching had given way to the kind of sharp, searing agony that makes you want to walk in front of an oncoming bus because *Oh God, just let me feel pain somewhere else for a second.*

My main reason for venturing back to Siena at this specific time is to take part in a relay race from Siena to the nearby hill town of Montalcino; almost all the contrade will be competing, and Dario has arranged it so that I'm running a leg for the Caterpillar. The course is eleven kilometers, and the shingles will likely make each step a torment. By such means do I prove my devotion to the Bruco. Prove it to myself, anyway; I don't know how to make anyone else aware of it without appearing boastful. It's easy enough for the brucaioli to witness Rachel forging her way through showers of molten slag, not so easy to perceive the lavalike burning going on under my shirt. I'm getting to be kind of an expert at this private suffering thing, for all the good it does me.

O'Hare International Airport is a roiling stew of travelers on the day of my departure, and my flight is oversold. I get bumped to a much later one but then upgraded to business class as an apology for the inconvenience. The plane deposits me into Bologna as gently as into a lap, and the train ride to Siena unfolds with equal serenity. Rachel meets me at the station and drives me to the hills above Vagliagli, up to the tree-shaded bench that Dario calls his office, where Dario himself is waiting with a wedge of Parmesan and an open bottle of Chianti Classico. There's a bit of a chill in the air as we toast my arrival, but it doesn't alter the warmth of the welcome, and when Michele drives by in his truck and sees us, he skids to a halt and joins us, bearing a bag of fresh fava beans that we shell and eat right there—and once again it's taken me no time at all to realize that I've once again arrived in an alternate reality; that I've left behind a frenetic world, rife with frustration and anxiety, for one in which the rhythms of nature still set the tone for daily life and in which pleasures shared are valued more highly than points scored or advantages taken. At Bar San Cristoforo later, Michele's wife, Maria Pia, joins us along with two charming expats, Nicholas and Michaela, and within minutes it's like we've been meeting for drinks like this every night of our lives. And at dinner later, Rachel prepares a meal with Dario's olio nuovo, still peppery and potent five months later and served by a crackling fire.

Maybe life isn't actually better here; maybe it's just different. But right here, right now, with the heat of the flames on my face and the scent of jasmine wafting through the window, that's not an argument I'm ready to buy.

~

DARIO IS OCCUPIED the next day, so I spend the morning with Rachel. She's offered to drive me to Siena but has a few errands to run first, and I'm only too happy to accompany her. The first of these involves visiting Clara, Dario's elderly friend, who is recuperating from surgery at the home of her son and daughter-in-law, just down the hill from Dario's house. Aldo and Luana have never seen me before in their lives but usher me in as though I've been through grade school with both of them and danced at their wedding. As for Clara—tucked up on a narrow twin bed in a room laden with artifacts both religious and familial—she once again appears completely oblivious to ever having met me before, addressing me as *gentile signore*—"kind sir." I mean, I'm a bald American with a big black mustache; exactly how many of those pass through this burg? Rachel, however, is a different story: at the sight of her Clara almost levitates from the bed, and the smile on her face lights up the room more powerfully than any rheostat. Rachel sits on the bedside and clasps her hand, and they engage in earnest talk. I'm left at a loose end; when Aldo offers me an espresso I gratefully accept, because fiddling with the sugar and the spoon and the little saucer beneath the cup will give me something to do.

It once again becomes clear to me, in just the short time we've spent together this morning, that Rachel has extended her sphere of influence from the contrada to Vagliagli; she appears to know everyone here and to have some kind of genuine interest in the varying conditions of their lives. Sadly, as Rachel's affectionate bond with everyone in Dario's vicinity waxes, her romance with Dario himself wanes—apparently the Apollonian and the Dionysian were just too different for the long haul; opposites attract but don't necessarily adhere. In fact, Rachel's next item of business is to go house hunting, for she still fully intends to move here, even though she won't be residing with Dario. In the ordinary way of things, the conclusion of a romantic relationship involves each partner's returning to his or her prior life—but even if Rachel were of that inclination, no one here would let her go. The more I see of her among the locals, the more apparent it becomes that they flat-out adore her—just as the brucaioli do.

It's a hard contrast to the frictionless demeanor I myself seem unable to shake, but maybe that's just a matter of gender. I can't imagine putting myself forward the way Rachel does—stepping into other people's lives with so little reserve or circumspection; in a man, such openness, such a disregard of boundaries, might seem not so much endearing as threatening. As for Dario, well, his riveting good looks and charisma rescue him. I am, I realize, pretty much on my own here.

And so it feels when I arrive back in Siena, which isn't till the following day (one thing leading to another as they often do here). It's a cold, damp morning; also, it's a Friday, so most everyone's working. I run into Giuliano Ghiselli in the street, which is about as close to a royal welcome as I could conceivably hope for, but it's my only significant encounter. (I do learn, from chatting with one of the locals, that the local term for shingles is *il fuoco di Sant'Antonio*—literally, "the fire of Saint Anthony." Everything sounds better in Italian.)

That night, however, there's the customary Friday dinner at the Società, and Dario and I go early to socialize at the bar. We spend some time talking to Francesco, a sharp dresser with keen eyes and a trim beard who's currently one of the mangini—the pair of assistants to the captain—and who Dario thinks may be elected captain himself after Gianni steps down. It's a little alarming that people have begun to think of Gianni's retiring; but he *has* brought home three victories, which is more than most captains manage in the course of their careers.

It's April, which makes this officially the run-up to Palio time. There are still two months to go, but already there's an obsessive interest in which contrade have claims on which jockeys; what each is paying or willing to pay, either for a victory or to prevent someone else's victory; the contingencies that will have to be considered once the final three contrade are drawn. It will become the subject of increasing inspection, dissection, speculation, and argument over the coming weeks.

A few minutes later Rachel walks in, looking absolutely smashing and bearing (of course) a bag of gifts. A roar of joy goes up in the bar—if you didn't know what was happening, you'd have thought Siena's soccer team had scored a goal on TV. It's the first chance I've had to observe Rachel in this milieu in almost two years, and I'm astonished at the difference. After all, she started on this path at the same time I did; I can actually remember—it seems ridiculous now—her asking my advice in the early days, as if there were anything about these people I could possibly tell her. But since then she's sailed right past me; if there's an American Caterpillar in the room—and clearly there is—it isn't me.

Yet I can't begrudge her or even muster up much jealousy. She's my friend, and thus her triumph is mine, and I find myself rather shamelessly basking in it.

And though my own way may be more circuitous and ultimately less resounding a success, I soon realize I'm not entirely without resources. In fact, I find myself rather easily moving about the room, seeking out and greeting Fabio and Gianni the vicar and Giorgio and Luigina and several of the friends I made on karaoke night. And at one point someone reaches out to grab my wrist as I'm passing a table—and it's Silvia; astonishingly, I've reached the point at which she not only recognizes me but is openly glad to see me. Her smile of welcome is disorienting; I babble something incoherent, making, I hope, not too big a fool of myself, and return to my own table blushing like a six-year-old.

Over dinner (pasta with sausage, stuffed chicken, poached pears, and gelato—have I mentioned that they eat *very well* in the contrada?), Dario fills me in on the broad strokes of the Palio gossip. The Shell, it seems, is the favorite to win; it has spent a fortune already and has Trecciolino lined up—though it's whispered that it's putting a lot more pressure on him than the Caterpillar ever did. Also, its rival, the Ram, isn't racing, so it really does seem to have a clear shot at a victory. And since it's an ally of the Caterpillar and the Caterpillar has won so often of late, the general consensus is that it's our duty to help it in any way we can.

After the dinner the contradaioli, as usual, trickle back into the bar. But Dario, Rachel, and I depart together, all of us having long days tomorrow. Dario is working, Rachel flying back to the States, and I . . . well, I'll still be shaking off jet lag.

As we exit the clubhouse onto the street, someone from the bar sees us through the window and loudly hails Rachel. She goes over and has a brief, laugh-filled chat, then turns to where Dario and I are waiting for her, down the incline of Via del Comune, and signals that she's going back inside.

Dario and I continue our descent. After a moment he chuckles and says, "Rachel Moskovitz."

Damned if she's not.

One Day, Two Legends

. . .

☒ A FEW DAYS LATER I'M RUNNING SOME ERRANDS IN SIENA, and outside the imposing arch of Porta Romana I come across a pub called Bar Valli. The name is familiar; have I been here before? I'm almost certain I haven't. This isn't an area of the city I frequent. Since I'm feeling a bit run down from all my errands, I figure I might as well go in and have a revivifying coffee and possibly satisfy my curiosity at the same time.

I enter, and at first glance the place doesn't strike any chords. It's a nice establishment, with a big marble-topped bar, bottles of wine stocked like tenpins on wide shelves, a freezer of *dolci,* a row of video slot machines—and, of course, the requisite wall of Palio memorabilia.

A wiry, craggily handsome man behind the counter asks my pleasure, and I tell him, "Espresso." He serves it up a moment later, then turns his attention back to the day's paper. I take my cup and saucer over to the wall, and as I sip the steaming brew I examine the dozens of photos. Most of them seem to chronicle the career of a single jockey, and a framed newspaper article reveals his name: Salvatore Ladu, better known as Cianchino, who won the Palio of August 1996, ending the

Caterpillar's forty-one-year losing streak, thus at a stroke becoming one of the Bruco's immortal heroes.

There are photos of Cianchino wearing the colors of a number of contrade—as well as an article that lays out the statistics of his astonishing career: he raced in forty-six Palii and won eight (two for the Panther, two for the Wave, and one each for the Shell, the Ram, the Tortoise, and the Caterpillar), tying him for fourth place in total victories in the twentieth century. In each photo he seems to embody the fantino ideal: lean, compact, wiry . . . .

I almost drop my cup and saucer.

I turn back to the barkeep and say, "Hey! You're Cianchino!"

He nods, in the careful way you'd humor someone who's spent ten minutes staring at the big HOLLYWOOD sign above Los Angeles and then turned around and exclaimed, "Hey! I'm in Hollywood!"

"I didn't know this was your bar!" I continue. "I mean, I *knew* this was your bar, that is, I knew you *had* a bar called Bar Valli, but I forgot—that is, when I came across it just now, I couldn't remember where I—" He's looking at me with one eyebrow raised, as though I were a cat coughing up a hairball. So I just shrug and say, "What the hell. Give me a prosecco."

There's a very fine book, *I trenta assassini,* which profiles thirty legendary jockeys of the Palio, with text in their own words. Cianchino's entry is the shortest, just two sentences long: "An old fantino told me: 'Salvatore, the bread of the Palio has seven crusts.' Now I understand." He is, apparently, a taciturn man.

Yet he seems willing to tell me a little of his life. Possibly because it's a slow day and I'm a willing customer; it must also be intriguingly unusual to find an American interested in the Palio. But most likely he's receptive to my curiosity because I've told him of my slender, but intensely felt, connection to the Caterpillar contrada. "I owe everything to the Bruco," he says, nodding for emphasis. *"Everything."*

The first thing I learn, to my surprise, is that Cianchino is two years younger than I am. It's incredible to me that someone of my generation can already have completed the full arc of a career—much less a *brilliant* career—and then retired with honors.

What makes this even stranger is the way Cianchino, who's barely past fifty, keeps referring to himself as being the last of a venerable old breed of fantini—a hardscrabble, hard-living lot whose ranks include such luminaries as Aceto, Bastiano, and Il Pesse—the last of whom was his great rival. And this was no invented rivalry either, no public relations gimmick; Cianchino openly admits that the friction between him and Pesse—with whom he seemed almost in private competition for Palio victories during the 1980s and 1990s—was personal as well as professional. "I couldn't stand him," he says. "He was a great fantino, but off the corsa . . ." He shakes his head tellingly. Pesse, it seems, caused frequent problems for the contrade he rode for and was accordingly often beaten up; whereas Cianchino, ever the gentleman, ever the professional, never once had a hand laid on him. The two men were like oil and water.

Cianchino was born in the town of Bono in Sardinia. A great many fantini hail from, or trace their ancestry to, that rocky island, whose people are noted for their toughness. In fact, there are idiomatic phrases about the thickness of their skulls. (Once, at a picnic hosted by a group of Chianti wild-boar hunters, I sat across from a man who swore that when he was in the military, he could tell the Sardinians in his unit at a glance. "It was just a matter of looking at all the shaved heads," he said. "Theirs are *shaped* differently.") The Sardinians are essentially an entirely different people, not only from the Tuscans but from the Italians in general, what with their distinctive tongue and their particular surnames, which almost always end in either "s" or "u."

Cianchino was one of nine sons in a farming family. His father worked in Germany, but despite the portion of his income he regularly sent home, the family was so poor that they couldn't afford to keep a stable. "So I learned to ride not on horseback but on pigs."

Despite this lack of proper training, he was spotted by a scout from Lazio whose eye for talent was fixed by the boy's trim, compact frame—ideal for a jockey. He recruited Salvatore, trained him, and set him up in a career in conventional racing. Soon he was noticed by Giuseppe Gentili, aka Ciancone, the great fantino whose historic 1955 victory was, at that time, the last the Caterpillar had enjoyed. He took the young Salvatore under his wing and convinced the captain of the Bruco to bring him to Siena to race for them. He was given the nickname Cianchino in reflection of his benefactor.

"I was a poor, unworldly Sardinian boy," he says. "For me, Siena was a dazzling, magical place, like the land of Bellocchi"—a reference to *Pinocchio,* a story that has the same resonance for Tuscans that *The Wizard of Oz* has for Americans.

The first summer after Cianchino's arrival, the Caterpillar didn't race in July, so the Bruco lent him to the Ram contrada for his first Palio. In August, he donned the Bruco colors for the first time, but as luck would have it, his horse was injured in one of the trials, so the contrada had to withdraw from the race. The Caterpillar lent Cianchino to the Panther, for whom—in only his second race—he won his very first victory. At the time, he wasn't much beyond his twentieth birthday.

It was the beginning of a legendary career, though he couldn't know that then. He didn't win any of his next five Palii—all raced for the Caterpillar, which had invested so much in him and for whom he was eager to make good. The first time he wore the contrada's green, blue, and gold was in fact the most disastrous—and must have seemed in retrospect an ill omen for the following four. "I fell from the horse," he says, "breaking my leg and my collarbone and puncturing my lung."

The Caterpillar released him to race elsewhere, though he returned to it twice (in August 1982 and August 1989), but he continued to win Palii only for other contrade. His victory in the August 1990 Palio was perhaps the most extraordinary and thrilling of the last century. Racing for the Ram, astride an extraordinary mount named Pitheos with whom he'd been paired for the previous two Palii, he found himself late out of the mossa, with the Forest, the favored winner, comfortably in the lead. And so it would have stayed, but for a sensational domino-effect upset. The Owl's horse took a tumble at the first pass of San Martino, then managed to get up and get going again but stopped just before the finish line—which caused both the Forest and the Unicorn, which had by now rounded the track two more times, to plow into him as they hurtled toward victory. Cianchino, incredulous, suddenly saw the way clear before him and sailed by his fallen competitors to a completely unforeseen victory—even as the members of the Forest, who had already rushed to claim the prize banner, looked on in astonishment.

"It was a lucky sequence of events for me," says Cianchino. "If I hadn't won, the members of the Ram would have beaten me to a pulp."

"Why?" I ask.

He grins slyly. "Pesse was their jockey. But when they extracted Pitheos, I went to them and urged them to take me on instead. I had ridden Pitheos in two Palii, I knew him, I believed in him—and I promised I could win with him. So they set Pesse aside." But then Pesse went on to win with Pitheos as well—in fact, he did so twice, in the next two August Palii—which I think must be one of the causes of the bad blood between them. At the very least, it can't have *helped*.

The story of Cianchino's 1996 win is almost equally astonishing. He was slated to race for the Caterpillar in July, but in the *prova generale*—the trial the *night before the day of the Palio*—he fell and broke his leg. It was as if he were repeating his first, bone-crushing performance for the contrada. As you can imagine, the dinner at Società L'Alba afterward was held in appalled silence, and when Riccardo the captain appeared at midnight with the hastily recruited replacement, the effort to feign enthusiasm was excruciating. There was no victory the next day.

A month later, Cianchino had not only completely recovered but climbed atop the great horse Rose Rosa and rode on to claim the first Bruco banner in forty-one years—the victory he had longed for seventeen years to give it.

It was, alas, Cianchino's last triumph; and perhaps sensing

this, he declined to ride for the Caterpillar again—believing it better to end his association with the Bruco on a high note. Though in a sense it wasn't the end at all; he had his sons baptized in the contrada, and one of them, Alessio, is now barbaresco alongside Bani. It's a measure of how completely his father's legend has saturated the contrada, that he too is called Cianchino—"Cianca" for short.

In 2005, Cianchino decided to retire from racing altogether, having noted the coming of a new generation of fantini—Trecciolino and his contemporaries—who he felt were handled more like commodities than members of the community. He wasn't comfortable in such an environment, so he hung up his saddle (metaphorically speaking, since his career was predominantly bareback) and opened his bar. In which he now is seated, patiently enduring my many questions.

Wary of wearing out my welcome, I thank him warmly and make my way to the door. As I take one last look at the wall of photos, I can suddenly hear the cries of the crowd, smell the tang of perspiration, and feel the earth tremble beneath my feet.

I'm betting Cianchino still can, too.

~

BACK IN VAGLIAGLI, Dario suggests a walk up to the hills above the town. We start the trek and soon find ourselves enveloped in the quiet hiss and murmur of solitude. The climb is a little arduous, and at one point I step on some wild sage growing by the path, crushing it and releasing a potent, earthy-sweet aroma. Soon we come across a cluster of buildings nestled on one of the rises. There's a main house, a garden shed, a garage, a swimming pool—and a sign that reads VILLA ASTREO.

"This is a bed-and-breakfast run by a friend of mine," Dario explains. "Come on, I'll introduce you." There's an impish grin on his face that perplexes me; he's obviously holding something back.

We pass through the gate and knock on the door, and a few moments later an elderly woman opens it—trim, petite, in slacks and a sweater and fully made up. She greets Dario warmly, and when he introduces me she offers her hand with genteel primness. Dario gives me a look, as if to say, *So?* All of a sudden it hits me: despite her age, I recognize the woman's singular features: the wide eyes, the aristocratic nose. "Rompicollo?" I whisper. He nods.

Rompicollo (which means "breakneck") is the fantino name of Rosanna Bonelli, who in August 1957 became the only woman to race the Palio (at least in modern times; there are rumors of some others in the remote past). I was aware she was still alive but didn't know she was essentially Dario's neighbor.

Dario asks if we can come in and chat for a few minutes, and she agrees, but says very pointedly, "I'm just waiting for my show to come on," and nods toward a small TV mounted on the wall behind her. She takes us into the kitchen and offers us a couple of espressos, and she and Dario catch up on local gossip for a few minutes, till she notices the way I keep looking around the place, which is packed with photos, books, artifacts, and display cases. "Would you like a tour?" she asks.

As we head into the adjoining room, I learn that the place isn't merely a bed-and-breakfast. "This has been my home, on and off, since childhood," she says, "so I've turned it into a museum, with each room devoted to a member of my family." The first we visit enshrines the career of her late husband, General Giulio Cesare Flamini.

The next room is dedicated to Rosanna's father, Luigi Bonelli, a playwright, composer, and general man of the theater; the walls are choked with photographs of his various productions, and signed portraits of his collaborators, including Pietro Mascagni and the great ballerina Anna Pavlova, whom Rosanna called "Aunt Tatiana." There are also posters and music folios from some of his shows, including one that—astonishingly—is called *Rompicollo* and features a young girl astride a horse. The look I give Rosanna makes her laugh.

"My life is interesting that way," she says. "Full of such portents. Yes, when I was very young my father wrote an operetta—widely praised—about a girl named Diana, who takes the place of a jockey for the Forest when he is made drunk by a woman from a rival contrada." Her eyes twinkle. "Of *course* she triumphs. Back then, the Forest—which is our family contrada—hadn't won a Palio for many years, so my father gave it a theatrical victory to compensate."

"And then *you* went on to live that story yourself."

"Yes," she says, obviously flattered by my interest; "though my own path to the corsa was a bit more complicated. And it involves association with another fictional heroine." She now leads me into a room enshrining her own career, and among the many ribbons, awards, and photographs is a splashy, colorful movie poster: *La Ragazza del Palio,* starring Diana Dors and Vittorio Gassman.

"The film is about an American girl who through various

adventures ends up riding, and winning, the Palio," she explains. "The director, Luigi Zampa, had been a friend of my father's, so he allowed me to hang about the set during filming. I was by this time an accomplished horsewoman and had even mastered bareback; I had always dreamed of riding in a Palio, as Rompicollo had, so this film greatly intrigued me.

"One morning the director called for six jockeys on horseback in order to film a scene of a prova. Only five jockeys could be found. I offered myself as the sixth, and he was desperate enough to accept me. So I tucked my hair up under my hat and joined the other five fantini in filming the scene. It was such a thrill—being on horseback, in contrada colors, on the piazza with the tufa beneath my feet! But afterward, when word got out that an uninsured young girl had taken part in a potentially dangerous scene, there was a bit of a scandal, so I decided to keep shy of the set. And anyway, what else could I find there to top what I'd just experienced?

"As fate would have it, the next day Diana Dors's stunt double was hurt in a fall, and the production manager was again desperate. He asked everyone if they knew how to get in touch with 'that mad girl from yesterday morning.' When they found me, they offered me the job of replacement stunt double—and so once again I found myself on horseback in the piazza! Though this time with a big platinum wig so I would resemble Diana Dors. Which was another strange coincidence, because the heroine of my father's operetta was named Diana. Like I said, so many portents.

"The filming went well, and then one day the production manager came up with the idea of generating publicity for the movie by having a *real* girl in the Palio. The film company offered to pay any contrada that would allow me to ride for them. My dream, of course, was to ride for the Forest, but my uncle was the captain, and he wouldn't allow me to risk it. Eventually the Eagle agreed; it had just won a Palio the year before, so they felt no urgency to win another, and the money was welcome to it. And just like that, I was accepted to race in an actual Palio! Of course, for my nickname I chose Rompicollo."

We've moved to a wall of photos of the event. There's Rosanna, in medieval dress, astride the mount in the historical procession; Rosanna, in the Eagle's gold and black, heading out to the mossa, crop in hand. "Unfortunately, my story ended less well than my fictional predecessors. I wasn't positioned well at the start but made up a great deal of time to reach third place by the second lap—I really thought I might overtake the others to win—but I collided with the Tower at the San Martino curve and we both ended up falling. The Shell won the race as I watched in dismay, and then suddenly the members of the Tower came onto the track and attacked me for having caused their loss. A member of the Eagle came to my defense, fending off the blows with a bouquet of roses he'd intended to give me."

She smiles appreciatively as I look at her with astonishment. "You mustn't mind it; I didn't. In a way I was glad to be treated as any other fantino would be. And later, some members of the Tower came to my house to apologize, because they belatedly realized I hadn't intended to hinder them."

She happens to glance now at her watch and experiences a little jolt of alarm. She leads me very quickly back through the rooms. "I tried very hard to find a contrada to take me the following year," she says at a slightly faster clip, "but alas, no one would bite. Still, I've had an experience no other woman can claim, and a wonderful life . . ." By this time we've reached the front hall again. She turns up the volume on the TV, and a quiz show blares to life.

I go to fetch Dario from the adjoining great room, where he's been watching a soccer match with Rosanna's daughter, Chiara. We return to the hall, where he attempts to make further conversation with Rosanna, but she offers only polite responses, unwilling to take her attention from the quiz program. She watches it while standing upright, shifting her weight from one foot to the other; and in this attitude she strikes me as rather equine herself—like a mare at the mossa, waiting for the race to begin. Quietly, we take our leave. (Later I'll learn that she's a lifelong devotee of puzzles, brain-teasers, and word games.)

It's been quite a day, encountering two such very different Palio legends, both still surrounded by mementos of their prime. I can't say they're riding on past glories, because there is no "past" in the Palio. Yesterday's triumphs are as urgently felt as today's, making Siena a very good place to be a hero—retired or otherwise.

AN UPHILL CLIMB

. . .

⚅ MY PRINCIPAL REASON FOR COMING TO SIENA THIS MONTH
is to take part in the annual footrace from Siena to the nearby
hill town of Montalcino, best known for its spectacular
Brunello wine. The two Palii each summer only temporarily
appease the Sienese's mad urge to throw down. The contrade
continue gleefully to butt heads all year round in an exhaustive range of games and challenges limited only by what they
haven't thought up yet.

This particular event is held in honor of the Sienese patri-
ots who, on April 21, 1555, left the city rather than live under
Florence-based Imperial rule and trekked the forty-three
kilometers to Montalcino, where they hoped to maintain the
institution of the Sienese Republic in exile. It's also held in
honor of Montalcino itself, which welcomed them with open
arms and with whom, as a result, the Sienese maintain a warm
relationship to this day.

Ironically, the race is organized by the Tortoise contrada.
All the other contrade take part, with the exception of the
Snail, which is the Tortoise 's bitter enemy and won't demean
itself by participating in anything organized by its hated rival.
Its place is taken by the Ruga, a district of Montalcino similar

to a Sienese contrada, which is friendly with the Tortoise and even shares its colors.

The course is divided into four sections, as in a relay race, and participation is supposedly based on the number of military units quartered in each contrada. The Caterpillar has only one such company yet is competing three teams—two men's and one women's. Dario and I are on separate teams, with each of us running the difficult final leg, the bulk of which is basically straight uphill to the gates of Montalcino. Our Bruco sister, running the same leg for the women's team, is Tatiana, whom I met briefly in the kitchens after dinner a few nights back.

I've trained for this like a sonofabitch back home, and my idea is to make a damn fine showing, if not actually win. The worst of my shingles has now abated, so it's not impossible. We head for the Tortoise contrada, where all the participants congregate for team photos and get their togs. Each team will be wearing running gear in its contrada's colors, and I queue up with the eleven other Caterpillar competitors for my kit. I watch as the team captain, a cheerful guy named Fabrizio with a wave of salt-and-pepper hair, hands out lycra tanks and shorts drawn from a large sack. Blue for him . . . green for her . . . green again . . . blue . . . and so on, till I'm at the head of the line. Fabrizio reaches into the sack and pulls out a great big of handful of yellow.

A yellow tank and yellow shorts. Bright, screaming yellow.

And I balk. For God's sake, I'm a grown man, well into middle age. How am I supposed to keep my dignity when I'm prancing around in *yellow*? I'm just about to request a different color, when it occurs to me that any salve to my pride that

might be gained by switching this ensemble for one re-
spectably blue or green might be offset by the harm done to
my reputation in asking for it. No one else here is getting all
choosy about hues. No one else is stopping to say, "Do you
have this in cerulean?" I don't want to come off as a difficult,
prissy American, and I sure as *hell* don't want to disrespect one
of the colors of the contrada whose favor I'm trying to win.
So I swallow my request, and my pride, and take the yellow as
though it's candy. I even say *"Grazie"* and flash Fabrizio my
very best smile.

But I really don't want to wear yellow any longer than I
have to, so while everyone else is suiting up, I keep my togs
tucked under my arm and just hang out. I consent to put the
tank on over my shirt for the team photo, but that's it. I can't
help noticing, as the shutter clicks, that no one else on the
three Caterpillar teams is saddled with yellow. Dario is resplendent in a very mature green. Ditto Peggy, the American
brucaiola. I get a chance to catch up with her as she goes
through her warm-up; she's incredibly limber—she pulls her
leg up into a stretch, and her knee almost knocks her in the
forehead.

We break up and pile into our cars to head to our starting
points. Dario and Tatiana and I ride together, along with a
friend of Tatiana's from the Porcupine contrada, one Guido,
the sight of whom gives me my first inkling that I might be in
serious trouble. His legs are absolutely ripped. Possibly, just
possibly, my plan of glorious victory might be in jeopardy.

We arrive at our starting point, out in the verdant countryside. Cars line up along the roadside, and runners spill out
and begin warming up—jogging down the road, then sprint-
ing back. There's a table offering water and tea and—God

only knows why—sardines. We mill about sociably, and I continue to put off the moment when I must don the fearsome yellow.

Though the course is divided into four lengths, it's not an actual baton-passing relay race; apparently that takes too long. Instead, each of the four teams has a staggered start time—the first beginning at 8:30, then the others at half-hour intervals till the last group, ours, sets off at 10:00. Afterward the times will be tallied up and the winner announced. When I notice the other runners beginning to congregate around the starting line, I check my watch: ten minutes to go. Time, finally, to suit up.

I head back to Dario's car, strip down, and toss my clothes onto his backseat. Then I slip on the tank and pin my number onto the chest—thereby reducing the acreage of sheer yellow. And then I unfold the shorts.

It becomes immediately apparent that I should have given them at least a cursory inspection earlier. Because they are, these shorts, very short indeed. Very, very short. In fact, my first reaction on seeing them is to exclaim aloud, "What am I, *eleven*?"

I have a moment of panic, because I'm well and truly stuck here. I can't go back to Siena for an exchange—even if I could, Fabrizio would be long gone by now—and I can't run in my jeans. I have no recourse but to wear these dinky little hot pants.

I'm just about to slip them on when I notice that, unlike every pair of running shorts I've ever seen, they have no mesh pouch to cradle the Essential You. They're just fabric all the way around. Sheer, yellow, peek-a-boo-I-see-right-through fabric.

I could end up making more of an impression on the contrada than I ever dreamed. But instead I decide that the better part of valor is to wear my boxer briefs beneath the shorts.

But wouldn't you know, my underwear is actually *larger than what it's underneath*. So that I have to tuck it up so it doesn't hang out, making the shorts look like a large yellow diaper.

Even more mortifying, when I drop the shirt it falls below the hemline of the shorts, making it look like I'm wearing no pants at all. I tuck the back of the shirt inside the waistband, to forestall any such misunderstanding by onlookers. At this point I'm wondering if anyone would notice if I just stayed behind the car and didn't race at all, because my confidence has been busted down to subzero. But I force myself to man up. "How bad can it really be?" I say, and I back up and look at my reflection in the van's window.

"Oh, my God," I exclaim, "I look like a pedophile."

There's just so much *thigh*. I generally think that a man has no business baring his upper legs in public past a certain age. (That age being, oh, fourteen.)

But I put up a brave front and go out to mill among my colleagues. Possibly I can lose myself in their number. And if this beautiful landscape of Brunello wine country should crack wide open and swallow me up? That would be okay too.

As I approach, Dario turns, and there's just a momentary glint of alarm in his eyes; but ever the gentleman, he immediately hides it and says, "So, you ready to race?"

"Yes," I reply. "Tell me the truth, I look like a pedophile, don't I?"

He cocks his head and makes a little dubious rocking gesture with his hand, which is very far from the ringing denunciation I'd hoped for.

But there's no more time to dwell on how seedy I look, because the official with the stopwatch is counting down the final seconds. Suddenly we're *on*.

I'm near the back of the pack, but that's all right, because I have a strategy. While everyone else shoots off like a rocket, I'm going to keep a nice, steady pace and wait for the hot dogs to lose their steam and fall back. Then I'll chug right by them to victory.

Except no one falls back.

In fact, after the majority of the runners take the first bend in the road, nearly a mile ahead of me, I won't see them again till after the finish line.

Soon there's just Dario, a good half mile ahead of me, and Tatiana, a similar distance behind. Which isn't exactly spelling triumph for the Caterpillar.

I'm realizing something: all that training I did back home—running ten, twelve miles at a pop, with decent speed—means nothing now, because I live in the Midwest, a great expanse of utterly flat flatness. The kind of flat you get for only a couple of yards at a stretch here in Chianti, before you find yourself back on either side of a hill.

There are, I now discover, muscles that you use in running on hills that you don't use at all running on an even surface. It's an idyllic, sun-soaked, gorgeous day in Chianti, and I'm out among landscapes that inspired the Renaissance masters. And I am wearing yellow and I am going to collapse. Just crumple up into a big steaming mass of hairy white thigh.

To buck myself up, I force myself to think hard about those passionate self-exiles in 1555. When they left Siena forever rather than live as vassals of the Emperor Charles V, they took with them their wives and children and whatever household goods they could carry strapped to their backs or wheel behind them in carts. They traveled an ancient, broken Roman road and must have moved at a crawl. They were afflicted by famine and disease along the way, and many of them died by the roadside.

By contrast, all I have to do is run—unencumbered, on pavement—a quarter of the distance they endured in the name of liberty. That's all. And to do it *in their honor.* How can I complain?

This stratagem works well for a time, and I huff and puff my way ever closer to Montalcino. But then, at the foot of the hill atop which that city sits, resplendent as a queen on a throne, the incline—which has been increasing incrementally for several miles now—suddenly zooms upward. I'm talking sheer. I have to propel my torso forward as I run, and at certain junctures it's as though the road really is rising up to meet me.

The grade is so steep that bicycles can't manage it. A couple of cyclists strive mightily to pass me, their legs straining against the pedals, before giving up and dismounting, and walking their bikes up the road beside them like pack mules. Finally, my strength gives out; I can't run anymore. I struggle on at a walk, with gravity pushing ever harder against me. It's as though someone has tipped the whole world up fifteen degrees.

And that's when I hear myself being hailed from behind: "Ciao, Robert!" I turn and see Tatiana, coming up fast—or relatively fast, anyway. Tatiana, who has clearly adopted my strategy of keeping a steady pace and waiting for others to fall behind. Except I'm the only one who's obliged her.

Well, I can't let myself be shown up like this—my one comfort, up to now, was that at least with Tatiana behind me, I wouldn't come in dead last. But Tatiana's not behind me anymore; she's right next to me, looking remarkably fresh and actually being rather chatty. I force myself into a trot again, just to keep up with her, and my calves start screaming like baby seals.

I'm so delirious with the effort that I can barely hear a word Tatiana is saying to me (not to mention that my yellow shorts have ridden even higher up my thighs). When we finally reach the city gate, I'm nearly ecstatic with relief; but once we're through it, it becomes apparent that we still have a way to go. The finish is all the way at the summit, on the central piazza. I may need triage by then.

Eventually the finish line comes into view, and I say to Tatiana, "Let's cross it at the same time, so neither of us has to be last." Tatiana cheerfully agrees to this face-saving scheme, and we sail over the line with the élan of synchronized swimmers. But almost immediately an official descends on us with a clipboard, asking to know which of us crossed first.

"Neither," I say. "We finished together."

He shakes his head sadly. "Sorry, we must have a ranking." In other words, *we must know who is the loser*. I'm so impressed by this bracing political incorrectness—in America, we go out of our way to make sure no loser is ever forced to confront his loserhood—that I happily volunteer to take the fall. For her part, Tatiana seems content to let me.

I ask the official who came in first; he names someone I

don't know, then points this paragon out to me—a gaunt, silver-haired, middle-aged guy who's celebrating his victory with a cup of wine and a cigarette. Our carmate Guido, it appears, came in second.

They and all the other runners—most of whom look at us as if they've been here since last Tuesday—are enjoying themselves as though at a party. And Dario did in fact reassure me that there'd be food and drink at the finish. I go now in search of it and find a table barren of everything but oily paper liners and, almost lost in a corner, one lonely remaining sandwich. I decide that since I willingly took last place, I should get the last food item, and I snatch it up quickly. I've got half of it down before I realize this may have been a mistake. My body is severely traumatized, and now I'm shoving a large mass into it with the benefit of only minimal chewing. For a moment, I think the sandwich just might come right back up again. Which, along with my last-place ranking, would be guaranteed to make the contradaioli remember me—though not exactly in the way I'd envisioned.

I managed to keep body, soul, and sandwich together but suddenly realize I have an even bigger problem. It was warm in the valley below, where we started; but Montalcino is at a significantly higher elevation. And I now notice that all the other runners have been met here by loved ones who've brought warm clothes for them to wear over their running gear. Even Dario, I now notice (how had it escaped me before?) ran the course with a shirt tied around his waist, which he then slipped on at the finish. I alone am bare of limb. And beginning to shiver.

But I can't leave yet; I have to wait for a ride back to

Dario's car. It's then that I spot a large wall along one side of the street that's directly facing the sun. I approach it, squeeze between two cars to reach it, and then press my back against the brick surface to absorb the warmth. This position also serves to keep me fairly well hidden from view. Though at one point a couple of well-dressed Montalcino women pass by (wearing toasty leather jackets), and one of them glances at me, does a double take—then turns to her companion, whispers in her ear; and she, too, looks over her shoulder at me. I can just imagine what was said: "Am I dreaming, or is there a yellow pedophile hanging on that wall like a lizard?"

That night, Dario rents the movie *Everest* as a kind of joke. We watch it over dinner, and I find myself thinking, yeah, sure, those guys had it tougher than I did. But they didn't have to *run* all the way up the mountain face, did they. And they didn't have to do it dressed like Tonya Harding.

Later, as I try to sleep, my mind keeps returning to the Sienese self-exiles who sacrificed so much to reach Montalcino. They had a motto: *Ubi cives, ibi patria.* Where one's people are, one's country is. What a stirring paean to citizenship—to community! I suppose that, in a nutshell, is what originally attracted me—still attracts me—to these people. But it's also what stands between us. This day has been a depressing metaphor for all the time I've spent here: running harder than ever and still falling behind, standing to one side while others celebrate and commingle.

I have one last chance to get it right. My life has changed; the world has changed. My freelance clients have fallen steadily away, and the banking collapse has evaporated most of my savings. Paying the mortgage has become something akin to a blood sport. If I'm to survive this, I need to commit myself to rebuilding both my business and my finances. I can no longer afford the luxury of chasing after the ideal society.

I'll come back one final time, for the July Palio, and do my best to participate fully—to be a brucaiolo both in spirit and in flesh; to be *present* for the event as completely as possible for a poor, moonstruck *straniero*. If I can do that, perhaps I can satisfy this longing from my heart; if I can, for a day, lose myself in the tide of community that rolls up from the Piazza del Campo, through Via dei Rossi, and down Via del Comune in a continual ecstatic roar, I'll have something precious to hold fast to; I'll have had, at the last, one moment, one blessed moment of true grace.

⚸

PART SEVEN

Summer · *2010*

. . .

BRUCAIOLO

A CATERPILLAR

...

WHEN I GET BACK TO SIENA, TWO TOPICS OF CONVERSATION predominate. The first is the Shell contrada. In April it was already favored to win the July Palio, since it had the best jockey (my good friend Trecciolino), as well as an enormous amount of cash to spend on "strategy" (by now we all know what *that* means). Since then, the final three contrade for the July race have been selected by lottery, and the Ram wasn't one of them, which means the Shell won't have its rival on the track—another signal advantage. The only remaining factor in the equation is the horse. The extraction is tomorrow, and there are two great favorites from past races: Fedora Saura (who has won previously, for the Goose) and Istriceddu (who won last August, for the Owl). Should the Shell manage to land either one of those, the race will be its to lose.

The second hot topic is the prize banner itself—the drappellone. It was painted by an Italo-Lebanese artist, Ali Hassoun, who has chosen as his subject Saint George and the dragon, with the Virgin Mary smiling down on him, all rendered in the style of the great French master David. But Saint George is wearing a black-and-white kaffiyeh instead of a helmet, and above the Virgin's head Hassoun has included the title of the nineteenth chapter of the Koran, which is dedicated to the Madonna. This has stirred up debate over the appropriateness of commissioning a Muslim artist to produce a work venerating the Virgin. In fact, the controversy has already attracted both local and national attention, with international not far behind. But here in Siena, the strongest objection to the banner comes from an entirely distinct quarter. As you can imagine, the Dragon contrada is less than pleased that its mascot is depicted on the banner as not only slain but lying in a heap at Saint George's feet. In fact, the *dragaioli* might well be said to be breathing fire over the matter. I rather like the thing, personally, but it's hard to find anyone else in Siena who doesn't have some objection to it, and I quickly learn it's best just not to bring it up.

This particular Palio is dedicated to the 750th anniversary of the Battle of Montaperti, in which the Sienese smashed, stomped, and pulverized the high holy crap out of the Florentines, to such an extent that Dante, a Florentine by birth and a poet by nature, exacted a writer's best revenge: recording for the ages his fury and disgust, penning that the Sienese brutality "dyed the river Arbia red with blood." The Sienese, far from being chastened by anything so effete as a few lines of verse, remain spectacularly proud of the victory, and even today, when they face Florentine teams in sporting events, will unfurl in the bleachers large banners reading REMEMBER MONTAPERTI.

I have some American friends in town for this Palio. Sally and Biff, with their teenage daughter, Grace, have rented a spectacular villa called Barbocce just a short drive from Vagliagli. Since I'm once again availing myself of Dario's hospitality, I'm able to shuttle over to see them shortly after my arrival and thus spend a lazy afternoon at their pool before plunging tomorrow into *i giorni del Palio*. Their son, Miles, is also on hand; he's been traveling across Europe with two friends, R.J. and Aldo, strapping boys who make me feel very old by treating me with entirely too much cordiality. There's also another family sharing the villa: the Hintons—mom, dad, two daughters. Factor in Dario's clients for the week, the Stouffers, and it begins to seem like a full-scale invasion. After my last few visits, I've grown accustomed to being the only Yank in town (aside from Rachel, who by now seems more Tuscan than American). I'm a little worried about how I'm going to immerse myself in one last, glorious bath of pure *brucaiolismo* when I've got my countrymen all around me grooving on the novelty of it all.

One small incident seems, on the face of it, a good omen: in one of the rooms at Barbocce, there are two antique engravings of Caterpillar *alfieri*. There aren't any other *contrade* represented anywhere on the villa's walls—no Palio memorabilia of any kind, in fact, just these two nineteenth-century boys attired in blue, yellow, and green. Later I'll report this to the *contrada* archivist, Francesco (aka "Il Tira"), who will be particularly intrigued—possibly I'll have helped facilitate a new acquisition for the Bruco museum. Which is a *much* better legacy than last place in the Siena-Montalcino or even second place in the karaokando.

The day of the extraction arrives, and there's a tripe and wine breakfast at Società L'Alba—which, believe me, is much more appetizing than it sounds and quite energizing too; or possibly that's just a matter of the almost palpable suspense. The brucaioli are humming with interest in what the outcome of the extraction will be, though in general they aren't burning with desire for a victory themselves; their last win is still a fresh memory, and in any case they've promised to help their ally, the Shell. But if the Caterpillar should happen to land Fedora Saura or Istriceddu? Everyone is certain that Gianni has one or two contingency plans in place. If handed a golden opportunity for a fourth victory for his captaincy, he's not about to turn it down.

Piazza del Campo is packed with people for the extraction, and the sun overhead is merciless; I've yet to attend an extraction in which the heat wasn't borderline lethal. I hover in a pocket of shade watching the ten contrada representatives, all in medieval dress (caps and doublets and hose—how do they keep from fainting?) as they await the beginning of the ceremony. One note of interest: the Wave has broken with tradition by sending a woman to collect the horse. She looks fetchingly boyish in the contrada's sky blue and white.

Though the heavens are scorching the rest of us, they seem to be smiling on the Shell, because it walks away with Istriceddu. Actually, its members march, leap, cartwheel— practically *fly* away. This is all they've been waiting for. They've got the horse, they've got the jockey, they've got no rival, and they've got cash to spare. The actual race might at this point be little more than anticlimax.

Dario isn't so convinced, because the other highly sought horse, Fedora Saura, has been taken by the Forest. "No one ever pays much attention to them," he says. "They have no enemy; they're the boring contrada. So they slip by under the radar. And that's how they've ended up winning thirty-six races. They could do it again, with this horse." The Forest's fantino is the twenty-six-year-old Silvano Mulas, aka Voglia (Desire), who's racing his first Palio, for which reason no one pays him much attention, either. "But he's won everything else, everywhere but here," Dario says. "It's a mistake to underestimate him."

The Caterpillar extracts a horse named Elimia, which at first I hear as "Elimina," not a hopeful augur. Our jockey will be Gingillo's brother, Virginio—which, again, I mishear as Vergine (i.e., "Virgin").

After the extraction, the only imaginable way to spend the day is in analyzing its results with every single human being you encounter, so we find ourselves at Bar Macario, where I follow about ninety seconds of the discussion before the speculations and arguments pile up in my head and I take refuge in a series of prosecchi. Then on to the nameless *sala da tè,* where in addition to the prosecco I have the pleasure of the company of Milo, a beagle who has the distinction of being the only dog allowed in Società L'Alba.

And then of course, on down to the Bruco garden for more discussion and a few more prosecchi. Suddenly I'm remembering the endurance test for the liver that accompanies each day of the Palio week. I'm feeling perilously wonky, and it's not even dusk yet. Fortunately, at this point a water fight breaks out in the garden, with the more raucous brucaioli squirting, spraying, and dousing each other with furious energy. I'm doing my best to steer clear, but eventually someone dumps an entire pitcher over my head, the result of which is instant clarity. Or perhaps not quite so instant; it takes me thirty seconds to remember that I've got precision electronics in the pockets of my now-sodden jeans. In typical contrada fashion, the very guys who assaulted me are soon helping me wipe the moisture off my iPod and iPhone and apologizing like crazy.

I'm invited to dinner at Barbocce tonight, but I don't have time to go back and change, so I arrive in a state of warm dampness. There's so much humidity radiating from me, I'm surprised windows don't fog as I pass. But I wear my sodden clothes like a badge of honor, because in the eyes of the brucaioli, I've graduated from utter invisibility to acceptable target.

The next morning, I'm only slightly less sanguine. Dario is busy with clients today, but I manage to make it back to Siena in time to watch my first prova, in which Virginio acquits himself handsomely. Then I go on to dinner in the contrada. I seat myself across from someone I haven't met before: Michele, a Roman blood pathologist who works for the contrada, monitoring the horses. After all this time, I still seem to gravitate toward my fellow *stranieri*. Michele and I have an animated discussion, because he'll be coming to America as part of an Italian contingent to the Kentucky Derby, and he doesn't know what to expect. I do all I can to convey to him that the Derby is so different from the Palio that it might as well be on another planet.

Luigina swings by after the dolce, bringing with her a gush of authenticity, and we have a long literary dicussion, about sixty-five percent of which I actually understand. After that I catch up with Daniele at the bar. It's one of my best nights ever in the Società. I've talked almost the whole night, just like an honest-to-God brucaiolo.

That's about the extent of the socializing I'm going to get, because the following night is the big *cena della prova generale*— the Palio-eve dinner that's the most attended in the contrada year. There are more than two thousand people in the garden, and Dario and I are again assigned the wine duties—which, this year, begin with unloading the cartons off the delivery truck. Dario suggested bringing along a second shirt, which is fortunate because the heat and humidity are so oppressive that I've perspired right through my first one before the truck has even pulled away.

My American friends are a little bewildered by my un-availability. I try to give them as much of my time as I can, but my wine duties are pretty demanding; Dario and I have about six hundred bottles to open for the dinner tonight, and we're armed only with handheld corkscrews (the professional wall-mounted opener is still broken due to an unfortunate mishap last year). It's especially frustrating because the wine was just bottled this morning; there's something dizzyingly absurd about two grown men working like maniacs to pull out hundreds of corks that were only just inserted a few hours earlier.

I do slip away long enough to escort my friends to the blessing of the drappellone at the Church of Provenzano; then on to watch the horses being led into the Campo for the prova generale. This is always very exciting, because the energy level is at about solar-flare intensity; but the bottleneck outside the piazza, where we're situated, proves potentially perilous when one of the horses quite literally kicks up a ruckus. No one is hurt, but you realize how easy it would be for someone to be crushed against the wall here—or trampled underfoot. It's only the innate sangfroid of the Sienese that prevents this; they seem utterly immune to any form of panic. For all I know, there's some folk belief that getting your teeth kicked in by a flying hoof is good luck for your contrada.

After the prova, we have a few drinks to cool down (the heat level has ratcheted up again, from hair dryer to blowtorch), then it's on to the big dinner. From my vantage point behind the wine table, it goes by in a blur; perhaps because we're so ridiculously busy. Before the meat course has even been served, people have sucked dry most of the bottles we've opened, and we're kept frantically busy uncorking new ones. The Caterpillar teenagers, who are doing table service, swarm around us waiting for us to hand them enough bottles to run back to their thirsty customers. Dario has brought panama hats for us to wear—a little visual signature—but I keep having to doff mine, sneak back into the storeroom, and shove my head under a running faucet to cool down. Either the heat or the pressure alone would've been enough to wring me out like a dishrag; in tandem, they've made me a gloppy mess.

While we're madly uncorking, I try to maintain some awareness of how the dinner is going. The atmosphere is relaxed, genial; no one has a serious expectation of a victory tomorrow and will be happy to see it go to the Shell. In short, the brucaioli seem contented to coast through this Palio. It doesn't even cause much of a stir when Virginio declines—probably due to shyness—to speak the few humble words that are customary for the jockey at this event.

The mood remains fixed at this even pitch; there's no escalation to the more extreme transports of celebration. Everyone is well behaved. Caio Buio passes out, true, but Caio Buio always passes out. While he's unconscious, someone draws on his face with a marker, giving him muttonchop sideburns, a handlebar mustache, and a Lone Ranger mask. When he comes to he doesn't realize this and wanders around the garden to the general hilarity of all who see him. I consider letting him know, but I don't want to spoil everyone else's fun. The next time I spot him, an hour or so later, he's scrubbed himself clean, and doesn't seem at all abashed. That's the way it is here. That's the contrada.

~

THE DAY OF THE PALIO ARRIVES. We pile into the bleachers; in addition to the group I've now come to refer to as the Various Americans (comprising my friends and Dario's clients), there's a group of bruciaioli: Paolino, Katia, Rachel, a few others. The historical procession proceeds as usual, with the hilarious exception that the Dragon has recruited all its ugliest men to take part in protest over the dragophobic drappellone.

Just before the fantini come out, Dario—who's seated behind me—leans forward and whispers, "After the race, jump over the railing; we're to help protect Virginio if he requires it."

I turn, somewhat alarmed, and ask, "Protect him from what?"

"If he's perceived as having blocked any contrada's jockey or helped another's enemy, they might try to take revenge on him." Perhaps seeing the look of manga-style incredulity on my face—you could park a sixteen-wheeler in my gaping mouth—he adds, "It probably won't happen. But be ready." What he's telling me is, Be ready to take part in a brawl.

I've only ever been involved in one actual physical altercation, which involved someone at a concert ending his disagreement with me over his place in line by ramming the ball of his hand into my chin. It was completely unexpected and disorienting and humiliating and, oh yeah, let's not forget, *painful,* and in fact it remains one of the most awful experiences of my life. Now I'm expected to be on the lookout for a whole mosh pit of that kind of activity and fling myself into it like goddamn Spider-Man? I'm middle-aged, for God's sake! I have expensive dental bridgework! I wear prescription glasses! In designer frames!

So how much do I really want to be a Caterpillar? Can I do this? *Will* I do this? I take a deep breath and steel myself. All right, then. Fine. Whatever it takes.

Anyway, here they come now: the fantini, riding out from Palazzo Pubblico, each one taking a nerbo as he passes onto the Campo. They all seem to radiate confidence and power. I remember that this year, for the first time, the jockeys have been subjected to a prerace alcohol test, though it seems to me the worst that could happen to a tipsy fantino is that he'd fall off.

There's absolute silence as the lineup is announced. The Tower is in tenth place—the rincorsa, who will determine by his own entry when the race begins. It's almost certain that he'll do so when the moment is most opportune for the Shell.

Yet nothing is ever certain in the Palio. After a fractious and nerve-shredding hour at the mossa, during which the riders and mounts behave with all the mathematical precision of bumper cars, the Tower inexplicably chooses to begin the race when the best-situated jockey is—his enemy, the Wave. It's a pretty epic fail, as the Wave takes an early and pretty impressive lead. I'm guessing the Tower jockey might need a little protection himself after this is over.

It's looking a lot as though the Wave might take the race, especially after wipeouts by both the Eagle and the Unicorn (hair-raising to watch, though no one is actually hurt); but here's Trecciolino for the Shell, coming up like white lightning; and though it's true that everybody does seem to make

way for him—the advantage of all that (ahem) "strategy"—
I have to say, it's a pretty goddamn impressive performance.
He just keeps thundering ahead; any faster, and he'd break
the sound barrier. Before you know it, he's bypassed the
Wave . . . .

. . . but so has the Forest. Just as Dario predicted, no one
has given much thought to that contrada, and without anyone
really working for or against it, its jockey—the twenty-six-
year-old Voglia—is free to go all out for the win, which despite Trecciolino's superhuman effort, he does, propelling
Fedora Saura right past the finish line.

And the Shell? Right on his tail—second place. The absolute worst of all possible outcomes. In fact, someone close
to me comments, "The Shell is covered in shit!" The looks on
the faces of the Shell contradaioli range from numbness to
shock; grief hasn't set in yet. But it will.

There's no lag time for the jubilation being felt by the
Shell's rival, the Ram—its members are especially exultant
because Trecciolino is one of their own, and thus his agree-
ment to sell his services to the Shell has been seen as a betrayal.
(There's even a rumor floating about that the Ram helped
bankroll the Forest's victory.) I like Gigi Bruschelli a lot; I respect him; and more than that, as an older man myself, I
would have relished seeing him win another Palio while in his
forties. But as it happens, everything has turned out wrong
for him; especially since Voglia, the young victor, is one of a
new generation of fantini who have come from outside Trecciolino's sphere of influence. I'm suddenly reminded of
Cianchino, who saw so clearly the writing on the wall that
ended his own career.

But I believe in Trecciolino. Having met him, I've experienced the quiet indomitability he wears like an aura. This can't be the end.

The Bruco's essential irrelevancy to today's events leaves me feeling strangely unsatisfied. Hell, at this point I might even welcome a bit of a tussle, even a black eye to wear home with honor; but Virginio finished so far in the rear that it's clear he neither helped nor hindered anyone and so needs no one's protection.

Back at Società L'Alba, I find it hard to keep up with all the chatter—the endless dissection of the race and what to expect from whom from now on.

I make my way around the garden, mortally offending two brucaioli by not remembering having met them before. I run into Peggy, and she asks me if I'd do her the favor of taking a photo of her and her friends. I agree, but once I have the camera in my hands I can't make head or tail of it. It's as if I've never seen anything like it in my life before. I might as well be holding an astrolabe or a Chinese puzzle box.

Even worse, I spot Silvia leaving and, realizing that this may be the last time I see her, I resolve to overcome my shyness and awe and tell her how much I respect her and how grateful I am for the warmth and hospitality I've been shown every time I've come here. That's my *intention,* anyway, but when I corner her on the stairs, it seems to take a lot longer coming out of my mouth, and though she's very gracious through it all, I have to wonder afterward what exactly I said and whether in my concern to leave room for people to pass behind me I leaned too far into her personal space, and whether in Italy they have the concept of the restraining order.

At the end of the night, a cluster of diehards has gathered

around the garden bar, where they seem to be settled in for a long, loud night. There are only two people working behind the counter—Daniele and Fabrizio—so Dario, perhaps pining wistfully for our duties at the wine table, volunteers the both of us.

At first I'm all for it, a chance to get some actual face time with brucaioli I haven't met yet. But I've never tended bar before, and I don't know what half the customers are asking for—or where I'd find the mixers even if I did. Nor do I know what anything costs. I can handle the beer orders; but it seems a bit of an anticlimax to my great Caterpillar adventure. I'd envisioned some tremendous catharsis—some great communal coming together that would sum up everything I've seen and done and learned. Instead I'm a barback; and a pretty lame one at that. *Humility,* I remind myself. *You're in the service of something greater than you are. You don't get to choose how to honor it.*

But I suppose that's in the nature of things. Familiarity dulls the novelty of even the most spectacular surprise, and if you'd told me, three years ago, that I'd one day be here behind the bar at Società L'Alba wielding a bottle opener and trading quips with the Bruco regulars, I'd have been dizzy with disbelief. But now that I'm here . . . I've seen how much deeper all this goes. I'm still skimming the surface; I'm still on the periphery. The extraordinary spirit of these people, their resiliency and honor, their loyalty and their pride—all these things are still only on exhibit, like the costumes in the museum: visible behind glass. I can see them but not touch them.

When the crowd finally thins out to a manageable level, Dario and I put down our counter cloths and depart. On my way out I turn and take one last look at the garden, still alight, still alive, still dappled with conversation and splashed with laughter. I can't even imagine when, or if, I'll ever see it again. Things have changed over the past few years; the world has become less friendly to adventuring. Leapfrogging the Atlantic every few months to come and pretend to be something I'm not is a luxury I just can't afford, in any sense.

And it breaks my heart.

~

MY FLIGHT HOME is out of Rome, so I spend a brief spell there as a kind of buffer—a period of readjustment to modern, noisy, gritty urban life. Though I have a particular agenda beyond just that: when my mother died a year ago, she stipulated that each of her children receive an equal share of her cremated remains, to be dispersed however we see fit. Since she was a devout Catholic, I've chosen to release my portion in the piazza at St. Peter's Basilica. This is technically illegal, so I have to be stealthy about it; accordingly I carry the ashes in a plastic shopping bag. When I reach the piazza, I bend down to tie my shoe, and while I'm crouched there I surreptitiously tear a hole in one corner of the bag. Then I get up and take a leisurely stroll around the Bernini colonnades, with Mom peacefully sifting out behind me. Then, not without emotion, I leave her to an eternity in the Eternal City.

That done, I'm ready to go home. The closure I didn't get from the Caterpillar, I've now had with Mom. Emotionally, it fits almost into the same space. Letting go is the main thing: that feeling of extending your hands and opening your fingers wide. Of giving over to memory what you've been trying to hold as reality.

I'm having a pizza and a glass of Chianti on some extraordinarily clamorous street when I get a text from Dario: *When do you fly home?*

 Tomorrow afternoon, I write back.

 Can you extend your stay a day or two? he asks.

 Possibly, why?

 So you can be baptized into the Bruco.

E*PILOGUE*

. . .

☒ THE BAPTISM OF NEW BRUCAIOLI IS PART OF THE AN-
nual celebration of the Visitation of Mary, which serves as the
contrada's patron saint's day. The roster of events runs in a cu-
riously backward order, beginning with an official visit to the
Caterpillar dead; continuing with the confirmation of the
contrada's sixteen-year-olds; and concluding with the baptism of the newborn (and those of us, slightly older, who are
to be similarly honored).

I'm so gratified by this unexpected distinction that I feel I
have to be worthy of it; and so, rather than sweep in for my
ceremony alone, I arrive in time to take part in all the day's
events. Dario, who's never participated in the funerary visit
himself, is only too happy to accompany me. We find ourselves at Laterino Cemetery, a quiet park of small mortuary
buildings and minimal landscaping. It's blisteringly hot, but
that doesn't stop the brucaioli from arriving in state, with two
alfieri drumming in the lead, followed by a nearly complete
roster of the contrada's officials: Fabio the rettore, Gianni the
vicario, Pierluca and Roberto the pro-vicari, Francesco the
mangino, Bani and Alessio the barbareschi, and Francesco
the vice president of the Società. But there's no address to

mark the occasion, no pomp or circumstance: on arrival, the members of the contrada simply disperse to stroll the grounds in silence. It's more of a social call than a civic rite; a gesture. The contradaioli move among the headstones and memorials as if to say, We remember you; we honor you; we miss you.

And then they quietly regroup at the gate for a bottle of prosecco and some pastries. It's all very civilized, even gently celebratory; not a mournful note is struck. As Dario says, "When you're in the contrada, it's forever. Even in death, you're included." (He reminds me that when the Caterpillar wins a Palio, its members bring the drappellone here to share with their forebears.)

I can't help making the comparison with the private, almost metaphorical rite I just performed with my mother's ashes in Rome; maybe I was wrong about letting go. Or maybe letting go is all you can do, unless you have the framework in place to do otherwise. Had I been a *bruco puro,* I'd still have Mom within the scope of my life; I'd know exactly where she was and would have a time set aside to go and visit her. That would be enormously comforting, but it is so beyond the scope of my imagination that it makes me a little dizzy considering it.

The ceremony is repeated at another cemetery, the Misericordia; then everyone climbs back into an air-conditioned bus and returns to Siena, where, a few hours later, most of them are again on hand, along with a choir and a crowd of onlookers, for the confirmation, which takes place in a large meeting room in Società L'Alba, adjacent to the museum. The juxtaposition is kind of thrilling: all those antique costumes and artifacts staring out at the lean, suntanned, bright-eyed sixteen-year-olds, whose casual grace can't—and doesn't seek to—hide their excitement. Once again, I'm deeply moved by the enthusiasm and commitment of these kids; they seem so ordinary, so familiar in many ways, yet their zeal for their community and its traditions is something absolutely singular. Each of these teens fairly springs from his or her seat to recite the oath of allegiance:

> I confirm to the directors, and to the whole contrada, my place among the people of the Caterpillar and promise to take an active part in social and civic life, with respect to the Sienese traditions that have been handed down to us by both constitution and custom. This my solemn pledge renews me in the ranks that these colors command, and in awareness of the honor of belonging to the great contrada!

There's no hesitation, no self-consciousness, no stab at irony in any of this. It's always seemed to me that the aggressive world-weariness of Western teens is born out of insecurity more than anything else; lacking a solid sense of identity, they put up a front of indifference, of disdain for instututions and traditions that seem beyond their grasp. The teenagers of the Caterpillar suffer no such affliction. They know exactly who they are. They always have. It's a fair bet that they always will.

Then it's my turn. Well, not mine alone. Outside, under an openly sadistic sun, before the grotto where Barbicone stands eternally brandishing his rapier over a pool of plumpish goldfish, the officials convene once again for the rites of baptism—in this case civic, not religious. Fabio, the rector, performs them himself, and he has about seventy before him today. They're conducted in order of the recipients' ages, and the first is an infant just five days old. Clearly it's going to be a while before my own time comes. In fact, there's only a small clutch of adults on the rolls today, of whom I am second to the last, just before Enrico, a tousle-haired athlete I met during the Siena-Montalcino race, and who is a few months older than I am. I also appear to be the only American; possibly I'm the only non-Sienese.

At last my name is called. I enter the enclosure—shaking Gianni the captain's hand along the way—and stand before Fabio flanked by my "godparents": my *padrino,* Dario, on my left; and my *madrina,* Silvia, resplendent in a sleek white shift on my right. It still seems incredible that Silvia agreed to stand up for me; I've never had a moment with her when I wasn't awkward or clumsy or foolish. Long ago, Peggy, my American predecessor, told me that the key to acceptance was just to "be here"; possibly she was right, and any lapses or deficiencies in my conduct have ultimately mattered less than the fact that I've kept coming back again and again and again—to be here, just to be here.

I look up and see Peggy now, smiling down at me from the railing overlooking the grotto. I smile back, taking this as a benediction from an illustrious mentor; perhaps somewhere above *her,* Roy Moskovitz is looking down as well. Then Fabio recites the few lines that welcome me into the fold and confer on me both the joys and responsibilities of being a brucaiolo; after which he quickly daubs my forehead, and just like that, I'm transformed. He places a fazzoletto around my neck and hands me a certificate of baptism, and Dario and Silvia escort me from the enclosure back out into the crowd.

At the final moment before I'm again reabsorbed by the

mass of people, I pause and look up, and there right above me is the window of the room at the San Francesco bed-and-breakfast where I stayed when I first started this journey two years ago—the very window on whose casement I leaned every night as I watched the life of the contrada parade by me—sometimes literally—in all its brightness and bustle and color and collegiality. It seemed at the time so separate, so distant; I could see it but not know it; reach it but not hold it.

I gaze up at that window and try to summon myself to it, across the threshold of time; to entice my past self to come and look down *now,* see where his journey will ultimately take him. He doesn't appear, of course. He'll just have to keep going one step at a time, one visit at a time, one glory, one folly, one throw of the dice at a time, before he can arrive where I'm standing now.

I can only envy him.

~

BACK AT LAST IN CHICAGO, I take my fazzoletto and my certificate of baptism and place them on a shelf next to my karaoke trophy. And there they sit like an exhibit in my own personal museum—evidence of someplace I went and something I did.

I set out to earn entry into the society of the brucaioli—to worm my way into the Caterpillar, as it were; I was patient and diligent and did not allow various humiliations to disillusion me, and in the end I was rewarded with a moment of almost spiritual commingling with a people whose life force burns so very brightly and with such irrepressible joy. The memories of that transformative finale will sustain me through the coming months of trial and retrenchment, as I turn my attention to the demands of a life I've left too long unmanaged in a world grown suddenly less navigable than I've known it to be.

Then, a week or so later, comes a text message from Dario: *Amazing! Gianni called for an assemblea straordinaria yesterday and announced that Gingillo is to be our jockey for three years! What an amazing captain we have! What a strategia!*

I can just imagine the rapturous tumult in Società L'Alba when this news was delivered. People would be shouting, applauding, clamoring around Gianni. I can see it almost as if I'd been there.

Later Dario follows up with an email, its tone still pulsating with the same urgency as his text: "This is the talk of Siena. The various contrade now can't afford to wait for the extraction of the horses so that they can choose a jockey. Very few things are certain. Trecciolino will likely have his second chance for the Shell, but his job will now be much harder; and if they don't extract a good horse the Shell might lend him to another contrada rather than take the risk. Mulas who won last August and who was disqualified in July, I believe will end up in the Owl again . . . ."

He goes on to discuss a few other possibilities, and I try to tell myself how funny it all sounds now, how remote, even quaint. But in fact I can hear my heart beating in my ears. Trecciolino versus Gingillo? It seems as though a real rivalry is being set up—a clash of titans. Part of me would love to see Trecciolino triumph, because if he doesn't, it might signal both the end of his career and a historic generational shift in the fantini. On the other hand, I'm of the Caterpillar now, and that must be, and is, the thing that drives my desires. I badly want Gianni to have his fourth victory.

"This will be a super Palio with a Bruco protagonista! Gianni is amazing! I know you only just returned home, but you must come back even so. I've taken no clients, we'll live the days of the Palio to the fullest. You are a brucaiolo now, your place is here!"

And before I know it, I'm back at the shelf, taking down my fazzoletto. My clients, my business, my slowly eroding stateside life—all that can wait another few weeks for my full attention. Jeffrey will just have to understand. Because I'm realizing that yes, an arc *does* have an ending; but every life is an arc too, and I can suddenly see the trajectory of this one. I can see it with great clarity, and there are no museum pieces in it.

.

POSTSCRIPT

I WATCH THE AUGUST PALIO NOT IN THE PIAZZA DEL CAMPO but on a small TV in Bar Macario among a group of rapt brucaioli. Despite having everything in our favor (including a very capable horse, Elfo di Montalbo), we know we're out of contention the moment the Caterpillar draws tenth place at the mossa—the rincorsa, which is a decisive position (since it's the rincorsa who determines when the race begins) but one from which it's nearly impossible to win. And so it proves for Gingillo, who despite a heroic effort finishes fourth. The race is won instead by the Tortoise, whose victory becomes the twelfth in the increasingly legendary career of its fantino: Gigi Bruschelli, aka Trecciolino.

ACKNOWLEDGMENTS

AS SHOULD BE EVIDENT TO ANYONE WHO'S READ THE PRECEDING pages, this book would simply not exist without the unflagging support, wise counsel, and patient shepherding of Dario Castagno, who is the best friend either I or the Noble Contrada of the Caterpillar could ever have. Anyone who has even remotely enjoyed this narrative is hereby encouraged to delve into Dario's own books on his extraordinary life in the Chianti countryside (as well as his beautiful *My Chianti* DVD), about which you can learn more at his website, dariocastagno.com.

I owe both eternal gratitude and eternal fellowship to all the brucaioli, who provided me with a vision of an ideal society and then warmly welcomed me into it. Among them, I'm most deeply indebted to Fabio Pacciani, Giovanni Falciani, Gianni Morelli, Giorgio Farneschi, Luigina Beccari, Giuliano Ghiselli, Claudio Bani, and my bruco *madrina,* Silvia Trapassi. Thanks to my fellow American Peggy Castaldi for her shining example, to Cristina Cinotti for Italian editing, and to Luigi Ravagni for kindly photographing my baptism.

Heartfelt thanks and friendship to D.I., for so many, many reasons.

I am humbled by the generosity shown to me by the

heroic fantini Cianchino, Trecciolino, and Rompicollo; I will never be able to repay it.

Those who wish to know more about the Palio and the life of the contrade can do no better than to check out Alan Dundes and Alessandro Falassi's *La Terra in Piazza: An Interpretation of the Palio of Siena,* an exhaustive and endlessly surprising study that remains the definitive word on the subject more than three decades after it was written. My own copy is very well traveled, and even now I keep it close at hand.

Thanks to Sally Turner, Biff Gentsch, and Miles and Grace Turner-Gentsch for sharing the home stretch with me—and for all the other indelible moments of our long and joyful friendship.

Mere thanks are inadequate for Luke Dempsey, my editor and this project's champion, and Christopher Schelling, my agent and personal hero.

Additional *ringraziamenti* for behind-the-scenes support and friendship go to Haven Kimmel, Augusten Burroughs, Simone Bianchi, Alessandra Addis, Clare Hennessy, Suzanne Plunkett, Lisa Hewitt, and John, Margie, and Iain Gayley; I owe you all more than I can say.

Tante grazie to Daniela Cavallero, who taught me to speak (and curse!) in Italian, and to Paola Morgavi, who graciously guided me through many of the language's great literary works.

Thanks to my dad for the Italian genes—and everything else he's ever done for me.

And finally, enduring love and thanks to Jeffrey Smith, who held house and home (and dogs!) together while I spent seven seasons chasing a beguiling and elusive dream.

ROBERT RODI was born in Chicago. After publishing seven novels, he released his first nonfiction book, *Dogged Pursuit: My Year of Competing Dusty, the World's Least Likely Agility Dog,* in 2009. He is also an active essayist, blogger, monologuist, and musician. Rodi lives in Chicago with his partner, Jeffrey Smith, and a constantly shifting number of dogs.